Object Lessons

Object Lessons

The Novel as a Theory of Reference

JAMI BARTLETT

The University of Chicago Press ❊ Chicago and London

JAMI BARTLETT is associate professor of English at the University of California, Irvine.

The University of Chicago Press, Chicago 60637
The.University of Chicago Press, Ltd., London
© 2016 by The University of Chicago
All rights reserved. Published 2016.
Printed in the United States of America
25 24 23 22 21 20 19 18 17 16   1 2 3 4 5
ISBN-13: 978-0-226-36965-5 (cloth)
ISBN-13: 978-0-226-36979-2 (e-book)
DOI: 10.7208/chicago/9780226369792.001.0001

An earlier version of chapter 1 first appeared as "Meredith & Ends" in *ELH* 76, no. 3 (2009): 547–76. © 2009 The Johns Hopkins University Press.

Library of Congress Cataloging-in-Publication Data
Names: Bartlett, Jami, author.
Title: Object lessons : the novel as a theory of reference / Jami Bartlett.
Description: Chicago ; London : The University of Chicago Press, 2016. | Includes bibliographical references and index.
Identifiers: LCCN 2015040307 | ISBN 9780226369655 (cloth : alk. paper) | ISBN 9780226369792 (e-book)
Subjects: LCSH: English fiction—History and criticism. | Meredith, George, 1828–1909—Criticism and interpretation. | Thackeray, William Makepeace, 1811–1863—Criticism and interpretation. | Gaskell, Elizabeth Cleghorn, 1810–1865—Criticism and interpretation. | Murdoch, Iris—Criticism and interpretation.
Classification: LCC PR821 .B37 2016 | DDC 823.009–dc23
LC record available at http://lccn.loc.gov/2015040307

Publication of this book has been aided by a grant from the Bevington Fund.

♾ This paper meets the requirements of ANSI/NISO Z39.48–1992 (Permanence of Paper).

For Bob

Contents

Acknowledgments

This book began at the University of California, Berkeley, where I was lucky enough to meet Kent Puckett. Kent took on the challenge of advising me on this project when it was about something else, and saw it through to publication. More importantly, he showed me how to write about reading with humor and warmth. That the book is complex, and that it is finished, I owe to him. I am grateful to Catherine Gallagher, Charles Altieri, and Michael Lucey for their rigorous engagement with the manuscript and its author at early stages. The remarkable work on nineteenth-century literature done by members of my cohort at Berkeley—especially Ryan McDermott, Leslie Walton Monstavicius, D. Rae Greiner, and Vlasta Vranjes—kept me engaged with the period while I read around it. Ryan McDermott read the entire manuscript, but even more valuable to me than the generosity of his feedback is the example of his brilliant prose. I believe that C. D. Blanton drafted the last line of the book.

Object Lessons found a wealth of insightful readers at the University of California, Irvine, each of whom made a significant impact on the shape and character of its argument. The members of my reading group—Andrea Henderson, Michael Szalay, and Richard Godden—did nothing less than make the project a book. The stakes of my argument, its contribution to the field, and its audience are in place because of them. My colleague Irene Tucker was a source of inspiration long before we met at Irvine—a piece she wrote on the state of Victorian studies that turned on a distinction between reference and representation was the germ of the idea at the center of this book—and she has been such an astute reader of mine that I will always be just a little bit starstruck. I am grateful to my colleagues Jonathan Alexander, Daniel Gross, Oren Izenberg, Michelle Latiolais, Jayne Lewis, and Victoria Silver, who offered telescopic readings of chapters that oriented the book as a whole. To Jonathan Grossman, I owe more than I can say. Jim Nyenhuis provided invaluable support as I prepared the manuscript for publication. Jim Fujii is a tireless advocate for causes big and small, and I am lucky to have been one of them. Laura O'Connor's passes through the manuscript allowed me to see its nuances and textures, as well as the value of letting them stay. The book rests, but never settles, thanks to her.

I would also like to thank the faculties of English at Boston University and the University of California, Los Angeles, for the generous feedback they gave at lectures I presented. Readers at the Center for Philosophy, Arts, and Literature at Duke University responded warmly to an early draft of the third chapter; it might not have existed otherwise, and it might be my favorite. It is a delight and a privilege to thank Alan Thomas, editorial director for humanities at the University of Chicago Press, who took up the book at a crucial moment and gave me the confidence to let it go. I am deeply grateful for the patience of my clear-sighted editor, Randy Petilos, who guided me through a swift and happy publication process. This book would not be an object at all were it not for Nick Murray, who copyedited the manuscript with exemplary care; Mary Corrado, who saw the book through the copyediting and production processes; Lauren M. Smith and her superb design; Joseph Claude, who kept track of all the pieces of the book and made sure it got assembled and printed; and Rose Rittenhouse, who has been assiduous in promoting and marketing it. Thank you to my anonymous read-

ers at the Press, whose curiosity and clarification made making
the book better look easy.

I owe my greatest debt of gratitude to my family and friends.
Without the support and encouragement of my late father, Jack
Bartlett—my first and favorite storyteller—I never would have
come to writing. He taught me to love what I do, and it shows
on every page. The memory of my mother, Sylvia Bartlett, in-
spires my own search for lost things. Growing up with a sister as
fiercely intelligent as Mindy Squillace has motivated me to stand
by my arguments, and to get to them quickly. Marina Olney will
have a story even greater than the way she tells one. This book
was written over several years of conversations with Talissa Ford
and Austin Grossman, and I like knowing that it still contains
some of their line edits. There were also some cats, and some
goldfish, and what happened there.

This book is dedicated to Bob, my best thing.

Irvine, California
March 2016

Introduction

My first most vivid and broad impression of the identity of things, seems to have been gained on a memorable raw afternoon towards evening.

« CHARLES DICKENS, *Great Expectations* »

The object lesson that brings the "identity of things" into focus for readers of the first chapter of *Great Expectations* is that descriptions have a false and fragile innocence, that to Pip the churchyard is simply "this bleak place overgrown with nettles," these "little stone lozenges" are children's graves, the "dark flat wilderness beyond the churchyard" is the marshes, the "low leaden line" beyond that is the river, and of course, "the small bundle of shivers growing afraid of it all and beginning to cry, was Pip."[1] Whatever viciousness lurks in the world that Dickens is writing his way into here, it is the referential practice that takes us there that is the most coercive.

Take, for example, the referring expression "the dark flat wilderness beyond the churchyard." The expression is a member of the class of noun phrases; it fills the subject slot of a subject-predicate sentence; other such expressions include proper names ("Philip Pirrip"), definite descriptions ("the author of *Great Expectations*"), indefinite descriptions ("a convict"), demonstrative terms ("this boy"), and some pronouns. When a speaker couples a referring expression with a monadic predicate (say, "smokes," or "is cold"), she intends to be taken as saying something about just one particular object, and thus the sentence refers in virtue of the fact that it indicates to an audience which object it is that is relevant—which object it is that is the "intended object" of the reference. But if "the dark flat wilderness beyond the churchyard" is coupled with a predicate like "was the marshes," as it is in this case, then the potential substitution of the thing that is being referenced for itself, its potential *self*-reference, points up the fact that thinking about an object doesn't necessarily entail thinking about it in the *right way*. What we get out of the referring expression "the dark flat wilderness beyond the churchyard" and the predicate "was the marshes" is a single thing that references itself as having more than one quality, or as being subject to more than one description.[2] As a result, our attention is distributed, transitive between the thing that is being referred to and the space between these two descriptions of it. It shifts from the thing that is being referenced to the space between its two iterations. My aim in this book is to infuse this space with meaning. Drawing on theories of reference in analytic philosophy, phenomenology, and critical theory, I take the act of referring apart in order to reveal the commitments, assumptions, tensions, and inhibitions that different references incur. I propose that if we can grasp propositions about and references to objects that are indeterminate in part because the act of referring destabilizes what is being referred to even as it infuses it with meaning, then the act of referring can be considered a crucial component of the way we process the literary.

In fact, we could plausibly read the first chapter of *Great Expectations* as an exercise in what philosopher W. V. O. Quine, in *Word and Object*, calls "entification," since both texts assert that the child's "first most vivid and broad impression of the identity of things" links objects to their qualities only through the act of referring to them. The marshes that appear at first to be wild become "just a long black horizontal line" at the end of the chapter when the convict Magwitch limps away; the "low leaden line" of river becomes "just another horizontal line, not nearly so broad nor yet so black"; and the sky above, "just a row of long angry red lines and dense black lines intermixed."[3] Here, our attention (and Pip's) is repeatedly pulled toward not simply the way things look and can be described, but toward the way that, as things, they are inherently referential: even mere "lines" somehow contain and communicate features that let us pick them out from within a world of many other things, not simply as a class of more or less undifferentiated marks, perhaps "horizontal," or "black," but as individuated, spatialized, and transformable objects. This is, for Quine, how coming to language works:

> Entification begins at arm's length; the points of condensation in the primordial conceptual scheme are things glimpsed, not glimpses. In that there is little cause for wonder. . . . Linguistically, and hence conceptually, the things in sharpest focus are the things that are public enough to be talked of publicly, common and conspicuous enough to be talked of often, and near enough to sense to be quickly identified and learned by name; it is to these that words apply first and foremost.[4]

But it is not only that Dickens's entified, sentential subjects stand out for us in this early fit of description. More importantly—and here is where learning the "identity of things" becomes so fraught and poignant in the novel's first chapter, as well as a crucial early index of character and plot—it is the very dynamism of these references, the way they solidify objects but also fail to determine them finally, that reveals Pip's capacity for action within the world. His effort to catch up to the way the dying light shifts the appearance of the landscape is linked up with the terrifying appearance of Magwitch: "a gibbet with some chains hanging to it which had once held a pirate" is described as one of "the only two black things in all the prospect that seemed to be standing upright"—cutting down into the long horizontal lines of the river and the marshes—and it is this that Magwitch is "limping towards . . . as if he were the pirate come to life, and come down, and going back to hook himself up again."[5] Pip doesn't acknowledge that his reference to the landscape is now further abstracted by a reference to which *no* object corresponds, and although the "as if" contains an implicit negative existential claim—a claim that there is in fact no reanimated pirate here—*we* know that just as the marshes are both brought into being and destabilized by the reference to them as "the dark flat wilderness beyond the churchyard," the landscape is entified by the pirate, and the pirate is entified by Magwitch, so that ultimately each of these objects exists by virtue of the space between Pip's references to them. These are the descriptions of objects that are supposed to get us to imagine the world of *Great Expectations*, but just as they expand that world through extensible referential connections, their objects fall out in denotation.

Readers of Dickens have not traditionally been critical of the linguistic evanescence of his objects. Citing Dickens's own claim—made repeatedly but never so quotably as in the preface to *Bleak House*—that he has "purposely dwelt on the romantic side of familiar things,"[6] we have taken the structure of his descriptions to be phenomenologically rather than ontologically mimetic, and understood their linguistic representational order to reveal a unique swerve of thought, visible at and attributable to every higher order of the text, from character, to narrator, to plot—even to the mind of the author himself. As early as 1856, Hippolyte Taine called out the "monomaniacal" penchant for pathetic fallacy in Dickens's work—"if one of the personages is happy, the clouds and the flowers are happy, too"—by inadvertently collapsing the grammatical distinction between the author and his objects in a syntax that looks sylleptical: "With Dickens, inanimate things take the color of the thoughts of his personages. His imagination is so vivid and eager that it carries everything along with it as it goes."[7] One hundred years on, Dorothy Van Ghent keeps to Taine's idea that the linguistic organization of Dickens's descriptions is "intuitive," the product of a "fantastic private language," but she does not mark that language as one that exclusively organizes in the direction of world-to-word. Van Ghent's historical position allows her to see these descriptions serving an "exchange function" in the novels as an analogue for the reduction of people to things under the advent of industrial capitalism.[8] On her reading, Dickens's use of the pathetic fallacy is no "incidental stylistic embellishment," but one half of a reciprocal metaphor: "People are described by nonhuman attributes, or by such exaggeration of or emphasis on one part of their appearance that they seem to be reduced wholly to that part, with an effect of having become 'thinged' into one of their own bodily members or into an article of their clothing or into some inanimate object of which they have made a fetish."[9] The effect of Dickens's "thinging" is a distribution of the inner life of his characters onto the novel's aesthetic structure: just as his bric-a-brac comes to symbolize mental states, so the coincidences of his plots express the latent order in human experience—what Van Ghent terms the "moral dynamics" that freight chance encounters with more weight than they at first seem to bear. The "identity of things" that Pip learns in the opening pages of *Great Expectations* is thus coextensive with his own identity: "What brings the convict Magwitch to the child Pip, in the graveyard," she writes, "is more than the convict's hunger; Pip (or let us say simply 'the child,' for Pip is an Everyman) carries the convict inside him, as the negative potential of his 'great expectations'— Magwitch is the concretion of his potential guilt."[10] In his analysis of the same scene in *Reading for the Plot*, Peter Brooks comes to much the same conclusion—that any question of who or what anything is in *Great Expectations* is expressed not by content, but by the grammatical form of Dickens's descriptions: "The repeated verbs of existence—'was' and 'were'—perform an elementary phenomenology of Pip's world, locating its irreducible objects and leading finally to the individual subject as other, as aware of his existence through the emotion of fear, fear that then appears as the origin of voice, or articulated sound, as Pip begins to cry: a cry that is immediately censored by the command of the convict Magwitch, the father-to-be, the fearful intrusive figure of future authorship who will demand of Pip: 'Give us your name.'"[11]

What is striking about these three readings of reference to

objects in Dickens is how strongly they rely on the grammatical form of descriptions, and yet how easily that structure affords analogies with consciousness, plot, and authorship. Taine argues that both Dickens and his objects take the sympathetic cast of whichever consciousness perceives them; Van Ghent collapses subject and object when she coins the verb "to be thinged" in order to describe the ways in which characters are at once metonymically reduced and symbolically enlarged via the intentional and progressive transposition of their qualities onto things; and Brooks takes Dickens to be using static, existential verbs to "perform" Pip's entrance into a world of "irreducible" objects via a language that is never existentially his. These arguments have informed countless readings of Dickens's work—including my own—due to the comprehensiveness of their vision of the novel as a distributed inner life, picked out and reconstituted in a single bound by the critic's own attention to the details in the details. After all, the grammatical order that is analogized into the descriptions, characters, and plots of novels, which in their turn analogize a phenomenological order, has its higher-order analogue in the critical practice that notices it.

But there is a problem underlying all of these readings, and it is this: *referring is hard*. Dickens makes this clear in a reply to Taine's criticism:

> It does not seem to me to be enough to say of any description that it is the exact truth. The exact truth must be there; but the merit or art in the narrator, is the manner of stating the truth. As to which thing in literature, it always seems to me that there is a world to be done. And in these times, when the tendency is to be frightfully literal and catalogue-like—to make the thing, in sort, a sum in reduction that any miserable creature can do in that way—I have the idea (really founded on the love of what I profess), that the very holding of popular literature through a kind of popular dark age, may depend on such fanciful treatment.[12]

In his association of the distinction between the fanciful and the exact, and the manner and the sum, Dickens cautions Taine against taking any statement of a thing "in reduction," and is clear that the act of "doing" a fictional world is a tricky matter of *deciding which thing to describe*, and *describing it in a specific order*, so that its components cannot be taken to be mathematically equivalent, or catalogued in a series of recombinable terms.[13] Analogues are what he is opposing here, for we notice that he offers no analogous figure as an alternative to that of the sum and the catalogue, but rather describes his (very literal) idea that fanciful treatment will "hold" literature through a dark age. So, what can we do with this observation? We can notice that the idea of "holding" literature as it passes through a dark age sounds like a refashioning of Taine's criticism that Dickens's "imagination is so vivid and eager that it carries everything along with it as it goes," and that this carrying movement is echoed, in turn, by Van Ghent's description of Pip, who "carries the convict inside of him," and then by Brooks, who reads of the origin of Pip's voice as the cry of a fear that emerges from his insides only to be censored by his father-to-be. All three readings are occupied with origins, and yet there is very little to suggest an interest in the challenge of choosing *what* to refer to and *how* to refer to it that Dickens considers foundational for the art of building and sustaining a literary world. All three make meaning of references without asking how references make meaning in the first place. If they took the problem of referring into account, they would see the ways in which they share in it.

For example, these readings take the linguistic attributes that separate subject and object to be coextensive with the ontological attributes that separate the latent and the manifest. This leads Van Ghent to make the argument that "Pip (or let us say simply 'the child,' for Pip is an Everyman) carries the convict inside him" via an infelicitous alignment of conceptual and grammatical logic: the conceptual proposition that Pip "carries the convict inside him" winds up looking like it is grammatically entailed by the proposition that a proper noun like "Pip" could carry the meaning of the definite description "the child" inside of it. A closer look at the semantics of reference would reveal that the relation of entailment she is invoking here, which stipulates that some propositions logically follow from others (the proposition "Pip is seven years old" necessarily entails the proposition "Pip is a child," but not the other way around), does not hold. The fact that Pip the character and Pip the proper name are not linked by a semantic relation of entailment—that, in fact, whether or not Pip "carries the convict inside him" has nothing to do with whether or not we could call him "the child"—turns out to have a fascinating impact on Van Ghent's argument. She is saying that Dickens orders the language of his descriptions to track the transposition of power from dominant to subordinate terms, and she is right to turn to Magwitch's domination of Pip as the first example of that transposition in the book, just as she is right to say that there is enough that is universal about Pip's struggle to locate himself in dialogue with another that we could categorically declare him "the child." What closer attention to the referential relation shows us is not that Van Ghent is "wrong" to take these positions, but that she is making a radical assumption about the structure of proper names: that proper names do not in themselves denote anything at all, but are really descriptions in disguise.

If *Object Lessons* could itself be said to have an origin, it lies in Bertrand Russell's theory of descriptions, which appears in an early form in the *Principles of Mathematics*, the first draft of which was, incidentally, finished on the last day of the nineteenth century. The theory of descriptions is most accessibly presented in Russell's *Introduction to Mathematical Philosophy*. That book, which was written for a general audience (the dust jacket pitches it to "those who have no previous acquaintance with the topics of which it treats, and no more knowledge of mathematics than can be acquired at a primary school or even at Eton"), presents the argument that Van Ghent puts forth above, that definite descriptions like "the child" are not meaningful references in themselves—they are not constituents of object-dependent propositions that need to refer to a specific child in order to be meaningful—but that they are meaningful rather as object-independent propositional *functions*: they express nothing more than "that which defines the property that makes a thing a so-and-so."[14] Russell's theory of descriptions is required reading in the philosophy of language for several reasons—his use of the analytic method is exemplary; his plain, accessible style is characteristic of the field; and his reliance on logic is creative and rigorous—but its import for readers of this book lies in the claim that

> It is possible to have much knowledge concerning a term described, *i.e.*, to know many propositions concerning "the so-and-so," without actually knowing what the-so-and-so is, *i.e.* without knowing any proposition of the form "*x* is the so-and-so," where *x* is a name. In a detective story propositions about "the man who did the deed" are accumulated, in the hope that ultimately they will suffice to demonstrate that it was A who did the deed. We may even go so far as to say that, in all such knowledge as can be expressed in words—with the exception of "this" and "that" and a few other words of which the meaning varies on different occasions—no names, in the strict sense, occur, but what seem like names are really descriptions.[15]

This statement has the potential to be revelatory for readers of the novel, because it advances a theory of reference whose meaning need not depend on any *thing* at all. The definite description "the child in *Great Expectations*" in the proposition "The child in *Great Expectations* is seven years old" is not a constituent of that proposition. The article "the" in the singular implies uniqueness, and so "the child in *Great Expectations*" only has meaning quantificationally, as a function that gives the following directions to anyone who wants to interpret it:

1. at least one child exists in *Great Expectations*;
2. at most one child exists in *Great Expectations*;
3. whoever is the child in *Great Expectations* is seven years old.

Russell is trying to advance the idea of propositional functions in order to eliminate our temptation to ground the meaning of propositions in their grammatical content. Talk about unreal objects like "unicorns" and "round squares" and "golden mountains" is made possible when we trust their grammatical position in a sentence. If we were to look for a definition of "Pip" in the proposition "Pip is 'the child' of *Great Expectations*," the definition is not to be found in the phrase "'the child' of *Great Expectations*" but in the definition of the proposition as a whole, which is "There is a term c such that (1) '*the child of* Great Expectations' is always equivalent to c and (2) c is named Pip." Now, since we know that there is at least one other child in *Great Expectations* (and that her name is Estella), we know that the proposition is false. At the moment, this is enough for Russell—he has shown that grammar is a misleading guide when it comes to propositions about existence, and in later works he will expand on the implications of this argument—but literary critics do not need to be told that the characters they write about are in some sense unreal. (Russell would stipulate that they are unreal *in some sense* because they could be said to be "real" in their own worlds, such that the proposition "The protagonist of the play *Hamlet* lives in Denmark" would be in some sense true.) What inspired the work of *Object Lessons* is the fact that (*a*) there is a logic to referential language that obtains whether or not it refers to anything, and (*b*) the philosophy of language is largely devoted to the study of that logic.

Having read Russell, we can see that Van Ghent's argument that we should call Pip "the child" because he is "an Everyman" is at the very least an imperfect paraphrase. Russell's position that proper names are disguised definite descriptions and that their references are propositional functions makes Van Ghent's thinking about proper names as *indefinite* descriptions strangely circuitous, especially when "an Everyman" was once itself the proper name "Everyman." It is clearer now why Van Ghent, Taine, and Brooks are positing the origins of subjectivity in *Great Expectations* through what Dickens called a "catalogue" of equivalent terms, a "sum in reduction" that misrepresents grammatical form as a form of exchange. They do this because the novel's opening paragraphs pose a problem of reference: How can Dickens utter non-denoting descriptions (descriptions that essentially *dis*entify their objects) and thereby say something meaningful?[16] They turn to phenomenologically inflected readings as authorizing the interpretation of the fictional world. But an understanding of the complex structure of referential language allows us to preserve the grammatical order of Dickens's descriptions—what he considered his "art"—while expanding our sense of what the language was designed to do. Brooks writes that Pip's cry is an entrance into the language of "irreducible objects;" we can now with some evidence suggest that they are not only irreducible because Pip cannot assimilate them to himself, but that they are irreducible quantificationally: they take the logical form of definite descriptions ("the marshes," "the graveyard")—just like the proper name "Pip"—and by suggesting their grammatical equivalence and their role as propositional functions, the form of the reference reveals that Pip's proper name, short as it is, can be reduced even further.

This is an object lesson no less powerful than the others Pip learns in the graveyard, and for that reason alone, a study of referential language in the novel is called for. But while this book finds a new interlocutor for the novel in the philosophy of language—and for the philosophy of language in the novel—it means not to displace, but to add to the store of literary criticism that treats the formal criteria of the novel: the objects, characters, and plots that are its content, the practice of literary realism that is its mode, and the ideology of form that constitutes its logic. The "antireferential bias of our criticism" that George Levine levels at poststructuralism in his book *The Realistic Imagination: English Fiction from Frankenstein to Lady Chatterley* has taken several forms. The influence of continental philosophy on literary theory had until fairly recently made the very idea of a reference to an object in language hopelessly problematic. The value that phenomenology places on intentionality diminished our interest in the role of representations; the value that hermeneutics placed on interpretation diminished our interest in ontology; and the value that semiotics placed on the sign diminished our interest in the referent. Levine's assertion that Victorians had always understood the metaphysical precariousness of their references and tried to work with the arbitrariness of signs could be seen retrospectively as the first step toward a more material account of the *language* of literary objects.[17] At the moment, there are many different ways a book on reference in literature could look, and this book is indebted to (at least) three of them. A book on reference in the realist novel could understand reference as a form of historicism, a situation of the question of what it means to refer from within the specific culture that produced the reference. Catherine Gallagher's work on the "failure of realism" in George Eliot's *Felix Holt* is exemplary here, in that it tracks Eliot's inductive, metonymic approach to realist description—whereby we come to know characters through references to the "low facts" of their material world—through her engagement with liberal social thought. The evolution of Eliot's referential practice from depicting life in the aggregate to ordering events and subordinating characters to those events is shown by Gallagher to reflect Eliot's interest in larger questions about what counts as the collective inheritance, the "culture" and "values" of a particular historical moment, and how determinative that inheritance is for the order of "social being."[18] Another kind of book, related in approach, would read reference for "thing theory," a critical approach that has its sentimental roots in the philosophy of language, pitching itself as an approach to the trickiness of naming, classifying, or apprehending things. Thing theory is relatively neutral on the ontological status of its objects—it is often lifted out of a Heideggerean vocabulary of "thingness" by a confessional style that moves between discussions of literary and real worlds—in part because its project is to show that things have the capacity to, in some sense, speak for themselves. Thing theory has argued that the culture that makes things significant creates the conditions under which they are received as such, so many of the works that belong to the category of thing theory historicize the reception of objects in order to discern why they pull the focus of those who see and act on them. Elaine Freedgood's *The Ideas in Things:*

Fugitive Meaning in the Victorian Novel suggests that the literary critical readings of things in Victorian literature—Dorothy Van Ghent's reading of *Great Expectations* is a representative text for Freedgood—might discuss the rise of industrial capitalism via the descriptions of things, but it takes things as a "bad" category, when, historically speaking, it might not have been so bad to be a thing.[19] Freedgood seeks out descriptions of objects in Victorian fiction that have narrative meaning on their own—mahogany furniture, cotton, tobacco—in order to show how not all things are equally commodified, but have individual, historically marked relationships to other, more capacious systems and concepts of value.[20] Finally, a book about the theory of reference in novels might suggest that the form of a novel is *itself* a reference, one that points to the ways in which literary forms take on ideology and are marked as belonging to and communicating information about historically specific social worlds. Caroline Levine's book *Forms: Whole, Rhythm, Hierarchy, Network* argues that literary works set organizing logics against each other (such as rhythms and hierarchies) in an effort to dismantle or denature the perceived permanence and totality of social systems and "learn how to work productively with them."[21] *Object Lessons* was inspired by all of these approaches to be a book about reference "itself," which is to say, about reference syntactically. The assumption that novels are engines of grammatical and linguistic reference that undergirds all literary critical approaches to the novel obligates us to situate reference prior to any other literary critical operation on a text and, thus, to think about the how the syntactic variables in the language of referring work to produce meaningful propositions about a world of things that exist only in the language that refers to them.

As we have seen, in order to find one of Dickens's referring expressions meaningful—in order to find any proposition meaningful—we must understand, at minimum, its referential context. We don't need to know whether Dickens is actually referring; we just need to know that he *purports* to refer. Most references—and here we could think of them as "fact-stating" expressions—are sentences made up of singular terms and predicates, so that the facts we state are facts about objects and their properties and relations. It is because of the familiarity of these subsentential elements that we are able to produce and understand sentences we have never heard before, or sentences that talk about unfamiliar things or states of affairs. In this way, the success of any language—its productivity and creativity—is effectively measured by the way its references are constructed. Robert Brandom argues that "any language with sufficient expressive power concerning its own conceptual contents—never mind the character of the world it is being used to talk about—must . . . at least purport to state facts about objects and their properties and relations."[22] So, when Dickens instrumentalizes his referential practice in the opening paragraphs of *Great Expectations*—thereby making an existential claim for the facts of the novel's world and emphasizing the disjunctive vocabularies available to the narrative— he is also inevitably cueing us into the fact that the problem of non-denoting descriptions is going to be a larger problem of his book. From its search for absent benefactors to its struggles with the intangibility of memory, the focus of *Great Expectations* is a novel that is pulled toward the conditions that make references meaningful.

Twenty years after the publication of *Great Expectations*, John Stuart Mill would claim that the identity of every object of belief or disbelief must assume the form of a proposition—say, "the afternoon is raw"—which he said was built of "at least two nameable things"—the afternoon is one thing and rawness is another—that may be *conceived* by themselves but are incapable of being *believed* by themselves. (An afternoon is nothing without its qualities; qualities are nothing without being instanced.) Dickens seems to be getting at something similar in these opening paragraphs: the linguistic structure of all of Pip's mournful revelations is motivated by the copula "is," which produces a relation that surprises us into conceiving the novel's world and recognizing the mercilessness of referential knowledge. But if, as Mill believes, the names of objects are simply their bearers, standing for the things of which they can be predicated, then identity statements between names that co-refer (lozenges and graves), propositions containing empty or non-existential names (Pip is shivering), and conceptualizations that are attributable to propositional attitudes (the sky is a row of angry lines)—in short, the entire *process* of referring that Dickens is exploiting to vicious effect—are neglected. Mill would say that Dickens's use of a proposition like "Pip is shivering" may appear to be a description of a name that contains and presents its attributes, but Mill's fundamental point about the practice of referring to things is that a proposition like "Pip is shivering" is composed of two nameable objects—in this case, one concrete and the other abstract—and that both names are used with the assumption that each denotes a unique object, and that in the instance of uttering the name, the x being talked about is that unique object.

The difference between construing "Pip is shivering" as an object that presents its attribute and as two objects whose copula is a sign denoting an affirmation or denial is the difference between a narrative structure and an existential structure, between presenting a relation and merely marking it. If there is a Millian representational system at work in Dickens's novel, then any qualitative distinctions that Dickens makes in referring to the people and objects that populate it must be read either as indicators of the psychological motivation behind the description ("lozenges" exposes Pip's innocence) or the overt textuality of the character as a construct (a "small bundle of shivers"). Clearly, neither of these approaches gets to the significant pressure heaped on Dickens's copulas, the fact that they enclose us within a novel whose "reality" is constantly revealing to us the constructive requirements that give rise to something like a sense of place. George Gissing's familiar statement about the beginning of the novel as a mood exercise can then be read as an effect of reference's epistemological heft: "It begins with a mournful impression—the foggy marshes spreading drearily by the seaward Thames—and throughout recurs this effect of cold and damp and dreariness; in that kind Dickens never did anything so good."[23] Gissing replicates not simply the order of reference from the marshes to the river, but in his gestural use of dashes, he also replicates this passage's shift from an elaborated to an abstract descriptive language; he even characterizes the referential act itself as a dreary spreading out of objects across the landscape.

A Millian reading of these paragraphs elides not simply the way that reference happens, but the fact of its presence in the novel itself. Reference is as much a character or mechanism of plot in these pages as it is a narrative technique, and yet to see how absent the question of reference is in recent literary criticism—and how fundamentally Millian our readings of referential descriptions are—we might look to Elaine Scarry's *Dreaming by the Book*, a philosophically inflected approach to the way readers inhabit the space of the novel by reckoning with its objects that comes rather close in spirit to the project of this book. In arguing that "fictional persons almost never misreport to us the tactile qualities of their fictional worlds,"[24] Scarry takes the position that the trust engendered by that fidelity to the solidity of objects, turning on a description of transparency over solidity—a shadow over a wall, for example—brings the room it contains to life and the reader into a credulous narrative immersion:

> Our belief in the solidity of these walls permits a phenomenon analogous to what takes place in the perceptible world. Locke says that in ordinary operations of perception, the idea of solidity "hinders our further sinking downwards"; solidity establishes the floor beneath us that, even as we are unmindful of it, makes us cavalier about venturing out. The same can be said of the fictional walls. The idea of the solid wall prevents not our further sinking downward but our further *sinking inward*. It provides a *vertical* floor for all subsequent imaginings that lets us perform the projective act without vertigo or alarm, and thereby lifts the inhibitions on mental vivacity that ordinarily protect us.[25]

Through her investigation of the strategies available to a reader who navigates her way through a novel's entifications, Scarry grounds her project in the kinds of questions about the meaningfulness of referring descriptions that we asked of Dickens and engaged in Mill. In treating the relation between real and fictive walls as "analogues," she neglects the ways in which our perceptions of fictive walls reach us not through our senses but through a text's references. Her only mention of a theory of reference—a line from *Culture and Value* in which Wittgenstein defines something beautiful as, "my hand feels tempted to draw" it—omits the semantic implications of what immediately follows—"seek your reasons for calling something good or beautiful and then the peculiar grammar of the word 'good' in this instance will be evident."[26] Her omission is conspicuous in part because theories of reference track projectivity and detail the ways in which speakers protect themselves from inwardness, but in part because Locke's substrate theory of "substance" is invoked as unstable and incomplete whenever reference theorists tease things from ideas, singular from collective particulars, ostension from description, and meaning from use. When Scarry later defends Locke from the charge that only an epistemological experience with solidity can produce its idea—he writes, "If any one asks me, *What this solidity is*, I send them to his senses to inform him"—she does so not by challenging the composition of the semantic machinery in virtue of which sensation is conveyed, but by saying that "partial judgments can be visually inferred."[27]

The wall itself is a fit place to begin thinking about the intervention that a theory of reference can make on our usual way of conceptualizing the "solidity" of the novel's fictional world. Locke argues that our sensate perceptions of things in the world are predicated on an unexamined, habitual, accustomed understanding of the impressions made on us by objects of a particular shape and size: "When we set before our eyes a round globe of any uniform colour, *e.g.*, gold, alabaster, or jet, it is certain that the idea thereby imprinted on our mind is of a flat circle variously shadowed, with several degrees of light and brightness coming to our eyes."[28] In his notion of the "idea," taken up by Scarry to indicate our "ordinary operations of perception," Locke incorporates a number of relatively disparate properties—sensation, experience, datum—and effectively conflates that which one has the impression of seeing and some sort of minimal, uninterpreted visual impression that founds and occasions all else. Philosopher G. E. M. Anscombe, whose work takes up the referential foundations of intention and sensation, argues that "when one reads Locke, one wants to protest: 'The mind is not employed about ideas, but about things—unless ideas are what we happen to be thinking about.'"[29] Ordinary objects of perception are, according to Anscombe, the "appearances" of the things we are inclined to think are there when we perceive the secondary, sensible qualities associated with them. The fact that when we are wrong about what we are perceiving, we can "retreat to appearances" like "it *looked* as if the wall was flat," or to substance-involving predicates like "it *felt* like plaster" is indicative that "the fact that something looks, smells, tastes, feels and sounds like *X*—or as many of these as possible—does not prove that it is *X*," and in fact no descriptions imply a substantial existence, and no sensible qualities can be immediately perceived to be the sensible qualities *of* something.[30]

Anscombe turns to the example of a red plate on which a light has been cast—to its surface variation, highlights and shadows, short streaks, particles of dust, a slope up its edge—and maintains that the standing red color, though its *esse* is not *percipi*, can semantically enclose variegations: "And yet I say with confidence that this is a uniformly red plate."[31] This reply to descriptions of perceptual experience is coextensive with Anscombe's argument about the paradox of many descriptions of intentional action. To the question, "If one action can have many descriptions, what is *the* action, which has all these descriptions?"—she intuits that we are in "bare particular" country: "*what* is the subject that has all these predicates?"—she replies that one should give *any* of the descriptions, *any* of the predicates. "Any one, it does not matter which; or perhaps it would be best to offer a choice, saying, 'Take whichever you prefer.'"[32] For Anscombe, an action or perception is intentional under one description but not under another: intention is not written into something inside the agent, and no descriptions imply a substantial existence.

Anscombe's decision to theorize action and perception as co-extensive confronts our tendency to imagine theories of reference standing at a distance from the kinds of instrumentalism and practical reason that Scarry is attempting to capture as the projective *act*. Philosopher Sean Kelly has recently pointed to the intentional reference to objects as the most productive site for the methodological interleaving of analytic philosophy and phenomenology—the former asking what part of the world referential language is directed at (invoking the need to individuate the meanings of various kinds of sentences in a language), and the latter asking what it is for sentences in a language to be directed toward the world at all (invoking the need to determine the conditions of the possibility of sentences having a meaning).[33] Kelly's reading of Maurice Merleau-Ponty's interest in the normativity of indeterminate perception positions him closer to Wittgenstein than Husserl, with whom he shares the idea that "we perceive objects as transcending what we determinately see of them and . . . that one project of phenomenology is to describe the details of this experience."[34] According to Kelly, while Husserl would argue that the hidden features of an object are indeterminate or absent to the senses, and the light and shadows cast over an object are not hypothesized but *sensuously absent*, Merleau-Ponty argues that "we must recognize the indeterminate as a positive phenomenon," and that "the perceived contains gaps which are not mere 'failures to perceive' . . . [but] *an indeterminate vision, a vision of I do not know what*" that is nevertheless "not without some element of visual presence."[35] Thus, rather than believing with Husserl that the light casting a shadow on a painted wall must be experienced as determinate and measureable, Merleau-Ponty experiences the lighting context as the background against which the wall is perceived and its color appears. Lighting is a discreet intermediary that "leads our gaze instead of arresting it," just as "for each object, as for each picture in an art gallery, there is an optimum distance from which it requires to be seen, a direction viewed from which it vouchsafes most of itself: at a shorter or greater distance we have merely a perception blurred through excess or deficiency. We therefore tend towards the maximum of visibility, and seek a better focus as with a microscope."[36] Lighting functions as a way of telling me how well I can see the thing that I am looking at, just as objects present themselves in such a way that encourages us to adjust our position and perspective to accommodate them. Determinate sense data describe and present the world, and the normativity that subtends the perception of indeterminate data is everywhere present to our reading of what conditions need to change in order to better refer to objects.

Anscombe says that when we are wrong about what we are seeing, we retreat to appearances like "it *looked* as if the wall was flat," and she goes on to say that if one sees a plate but doesn't see that it has no behind, and therefore is not a plate, the reference we make to "a plate" is a composite picture of a visual object, a true description of what the object one sees is, *as well* as a description of what it strikes one as. Intentional objects in both Merleau-Ponty and Anscombe in effect *deliver* to us the descriptive conditions under which they are intentional. Kelly argues that Merleau-Ponty contributes to Anscombe's analytic thesis the idea that perceptual descriptions are not founded on the presentation of sense data at all, but something positively indeterminate whose indeterminacy is the result of its essential normativity—its susceptibility to a referentially motivated sense of how well we are seeing something.

Thus, the projective act that Scarry says is ignited by that shadow on a wall in virtue of which our "visual inference" of solidity obtains—a view that retains a Millian understanding of the nameable object as a uniquely existent x—is unpacked by theorists of reference as an engagement with the contextual conditions that make entification possible. For Mill, the central use of propositions is to make nameable objects believable, not just conceivable, entities. For reference theorists, by contrast, the question of belief or disbelief can be effectively suspended or displaced onto the relation between objects and their contexts. In other words, we don't have to read the problem of expressing solidity as a problem of realism or the mechanism by which we suspend disbelief—we can instead think of it as an engagement with the conditions that make reference possible at all, an engagement registered not just at the level of object description, but at the level of narration, character, and plot. This book takes as its central argument the idea that if we understand objects of reference as given by phrases that describe how the object is seen by the person seeing it—and if we acknowledge, with Scarry, that novels are constructed by an engagement with objects—then we can develop the idea that the reference to objects is what is made by and what constitutes narrative. If we imbricate theories of reference and close readings of novel descriptions of objects in an effort to isolate the disclosive properties of these objects, then we can detach and make available those properties to an analysis of all novels, developing a clearer sense not just of what characters, novels, and novelists want and mean to do with things, but of what a study of reference has to tell us about a genre that habitually utters non-denoting descriptions and thereby manages to say something meaningful.

Scarry's ability to reinvigorate debates about the way we come to believe in fictional worlds, negative existentials, and non-denoting descriptions is grounded in two recent and interpenetrating trends in literary criticism, one ethical and one cognitive, that seek to characterize emotions as intelligent, discerning responses to the perception of value.[37] In her book *Ugly Feelings*, Sianne Ngai interrogates the location and aesthetics of negative emotions, specifically their circulation outside the subject, and the politically ambiguous role that they play in the social construction of our ethical dispositions toward race, gender, and class. Ngai argues that just because a work is ascribed, say, a "joyous intensity" does not mean that it *represents* or *expresses* joy, or makes the reader *feel* joyous in particular. She raises such questions as, Who is the subject of this emotion? Should this feeling belong to a subject at all? and, How is it produced by the object?[38] Her work is founded on the *grammar* of emotions, particularly the "aesthetic predicates" used by narratologists like

Gérard Genette and I. A. Richards (who calls them "aesthetic or 'projectile' adjectives"),[39] which evaluate literary objects in terms that seek to justify our feelings about the object itself: "Hence while disgust is always disgust *toward,* in the same way that envy is envy *of*—whereas it makes no sense to speak of stuplimity of or animatedness toward—its grammar brings it closer to the intransitive feelings in this study [such as anxiety, paranoia, and irritation] than to the other emotions with which it is traditionally classified. For while envy and disgust are clearly object-directed, their trajectories are directed toward the *negation* of these objects, either by denying them or subjecting them to epistemological skepticism."[40]

Ngai's work continues a cognitivist strand in the theory of affect—from Brian Massumi's *Parables for the Virtual* to Mark B. N. Hansen's *New Philosophy for New Media*—that takes us beyond our conventional understanding of the ways that literature engages our neurological processing of non-denoting references, as expressed in works such as George Lakoff and Mark Johnson's *Metaphors We Live By* and *Philosophy in the Flesh*, and Mark Turner's *The Literary Mind*, which have foregrounded the hermeneutics of nonliteral, indirect speech acts like metaphor as instruments that organize stories and minds. The more recent intervention in cognitive affect recasts the emotional aspects of literary response as a modality of embodiment rather than merely assimilating them to cognition; an inquiry into the perception of value is made possible when we question the source and composition of emotions as social (with Merleau-Ponty, we could also say "normative") categories, an act that makes them available to theories of ethics.

Other critics approach the affective interleaving of cognition and ethics historically, unpacking the political and economic origins of "value." Recent theories of the eighteenth- and nineteenth-century novel, for example, have tried to get at the question of how characters are integrated into their fictional social world by tightening the radius of relevant details around their socioeconomic roles. In *The Economy of Character*, Deidre

Lynch involves the novel in disquisitions on the image of the machine as a unifying record of a diffuse social system. She argues that novels value a character's idiosyncratic specialization insofar as it implicates those of other characters, thereby arranging a mass of individualities into a coherent social relation. For Lynch, a heroine's role in a "market of social exchange" results in the valuation "of characters who, as we say, have taken on lives of their own, even though our faith in their singularity and autonomy is difficult to reconcile with our knowledge that a character exists to be read, that the legibility of the literary character makes it a social experience."[41]

Alex Woloch, in *The One vs. the Many*, casts this act of arranging as a series of subsumptions, a "labor theory of character" organized as system of major and minor cogs working toward the isolation of a dynamic character, who is "configured as a distinct, compelling personality even as he is embedded within a larger social, and narrative, context."[42] Woloch ostends Marx's claim that utilitarianism converts people into functions, "abstract expression of utility," and argues that the realist novel's depiction of the "context of omniscient, asymmetric character-systems" tries to better illuminate the "proletariat" of minor characters by registering the way in which the progress of a novel's protagonist "is facilitated through a series of interactions with minor characters."[43] By explicitly invoking an economic model, Lynch and Woloch figure character as an *a priori* system and substitute that system for the character itself; when they do, they are led to the way that readers experience the social conditions that create the system.

And yet, despite the fact that both authors argue for a projective act that engages readers with systems of meaning that explicitly refer to characters as objects and to the compositions of texts as deliberate acts of reference, neither considers the tension between the characters depicted as objects and the objects that characters themselves pick out and engage with—a perspective that would reveal how objects disclose their own conditions of satisfaction, thereby complicating and illuminating the questions of self-presentation that both authors historicize. Also absent is a look at the novel's references to objects, including (as we saw in Dickens) reference itself, its ideas about the way novels actually refer. A reading of the way novels come to refer in the first place would have thickened Lynch's and Woloch's arguments about the origins of the projective act and grounded their characterologies in the normativity of representation that makes social construction possible. Their methodologies replicate the strategies (and the limitations) of cognitivism in their assertion that characters are productive of and embodied by intransitive terms that build on the negations of their objects: the character can only become a character-system, and the character-system a series of interpretative avenues whose focus must be pulled by the evacuation (and thus the internal development) of protagonists.

All of these ways of interleaving cognition and ethics into an affective approach to the literary—a theory rooted in a grammar of non-denoting descriptions—reassert believability as the payoff of a successful aesthetic experience. As averse as it is to the kind of cultural criticism that would reduce all objects to their status as commodities, Bill Brown's historical ontology of "things," which he defines as "objects that are materialized from and in the physical world," shares with the accounts of Scarry, Ngai, Lynch, and Woloch a desire to unpack the abstracted relations between objects that result in their believability.[44] Brown's effort to evacuate things of their interiority, both in order to "arrest language's wish, as described by Michel Serres, that the 'whole world derive from language'"[45] and to "arrest [objects'] doubleness, their vertiginous capacity to be both things and signs,"[46] remains an attempt to entify commodification, to posit a referential act that turns the things we have acquired into the things that we identify with. Brown insists on the contingent individuality of people and their objects, and argues that, when it comes to fetishism in particular, "neither [with] the 'object lessons' *in* the period nor cultural histories *of* the period, neither by the paradigms of consumption provided by Zola and Dreiser nor by historical accounts of consumerism" can we capture the "metaphysical subtleties" that subtend the ways in which we perceive and refer to objects.[47] One of the primary tensions in Brown's work is what Charles Altieri calls its stress on the delimitations of imagination to organize our relation to objects, "however much that work is objectified by social structures":[48]

> A large part of his project involves a modernist setting the imagination against its own idealizations so that it can bring out what is different in the life of things, and hence what is lost when we idealize things as the stuff of symbols and metaphors. But at the same time he wants to concentrate on how that life of things becomes a problematic and dynamic force as it provokes and sponsors social constructions. He wants simultaneously to study how things present states that are valuable because they resist human making and how things matter in relation to what society makes of them. The tension between these two goals can be resolved only by emphasizing various aspects of the uncanny where things get to maintain their otherness even or especially when we try to turn them into objects.[49]

In a way, Brown's problem is the one that preoccupies Anscombe—"Is there not a description which gives simply what is *seen*—and does not depend on whether one or another thing which can't possibly be being seen is the case?"[50]—and leads her to the conclusion that any ordinary object of perception "*has to be understood as a picture of* a purely visual object."[51] This is a struggle for the instantaneous self-presentation of things as grasped, for things whose descriptions hand over their status as intentional, over and against what Altieri calls the latency of Brown's understanding of thingness (the unformed object) and its excess (that which remains irreducible to objects).[52]

Each of these critics mobilizes theories of reference while treating the referential act as an unanalyzable simple. Scarry entifies the novel's nameable objects; Ngai aligns the diffuse power of negative affect with intransitive verbs; Woloch and Lynch depict asymmetric character-systems and social machines as isometric indexes of character legibility; and Brown "arrests" language's wish to be the source of all objects, and objects' wish to be both things and signs, all in an attempt to show us that Millian propositions work, that references to objects (figured here as diffusely, reader-organized characters, emotions, minds, and "things") result in believable fictions. What they don't theorize is how reference happens in the first place: when it happens, who it happens to, what its conditions of satisfaction are, what circumstances obtain in virtue of which it becomes intelligible, and what goes wrong when it doesn't. The kind of work being done by theorists of reference in a range of philosophical schools—Anscombe and Kelly are philosophers of language whose methodologies usefully take up both analytic and phenomenological perspectives—addresses the concerns that underlie each of these projects, specifically the relations between objects and their self-presenting intentions, objects and our attempts to act on them, and objects and our references to them in language.

Object Lessons is an attempt to bring these concerns to the realist novel, and to consider the novel itself as a theory of reference. While we often speak of the claim to referentiality that the novel makes—it is the genre that attracts Scarry, Ngai, Lynch, Woloch, and Brown because it exists to describe things, and it is organized by a causal logic that is grounded in instrumentalism—we tend to take the *act* of "reference" as a given. If we think of a reference as simply the thing in the novel that points to a class of characters or objects in the world, a specific untruth that stands in for a general truth, then our eyes are directed at two sets of ends: the social conditions that produce this metonymy and the affective engagement that it sets off in the reader. My point of view is situated slightly to the side of this system, and looks toward the instabilities that surround and characterize the referential act. My subject is not the thing that is said or described, but the criteria that underlie the process of saying something about it. In each of these chapters, the stress of my reading falls at the intersection of two axes: the degree of coarse- or fine-grainedness of a novel's references to things, and the degree of immanent or transcendent information that these references present. This book follows a handful of authors—George Meredith, William Makepeace Thackeray, Elizabeth Gaskell, and

Iris Murdoch—who write novels that stage the philosophical problems of reference by writing through and about referring terms, the names and descriptions that allow us to "see" objects in the novel. I analyze particular kinds of objects, ones that analytic philosophy defines as "intentional" objects, because they contain descriptions of themselves as really or potentially acted upon. My focus on intentional objects in the novel helps us to reconsider recent arguments about subjectivity and character, and my view of such objects as existing within a web of intentions, actions, and decisions supplements and contextualizes the centrality of things in their various constructions of novelistic realism and believability. I have turned to theories of reference in analytic philosophy, phenomenology, and critical theory in order to show that understanding the novel as a theory of reference is not only to imagine the novel as a form of philosophy, but also to show that it has been exactly that all along.

Philosophies of reference have not made themselves available to literary theorists, or to the field of aesthetics in general. In many ways it is neither necessary nor quite fair to play up the extent to which critics share a Millian theory of reference with such philosophies, since they are operating under the same methodological constraints. I take analytic philosophy as an exemplary case here, since it is oriented toward the ways we use language to talk about that which is *not* language, and thus spills a lot of ink over the question of how non-denoting descriptions work. When analytic philosophers tackle aesthetics, most of their contributions revolve around first-order questions of truth-values, ontology, and entification; any second-order questions about the means by which these factors result in a patina of believability are usually diverted into evaluations of the *best kind* of truth-value criteria.

The first and only volume to anthologize analytic approaches to aesthetics—published by Blackwell in 2004 for the purpose of undergraduate teaching—*Aesthetics and the Philosophy of Art: The Analytic Tradition,* is organized by section titles like "Identifying Art," "Ontology of Art," "Aesthetic Properties," and "Fictionality," and constellations of subject-specific versions of the same, such as "Music," "Pictorial Art," and "Literature." (John Searle, whose "On the Logical Status of Fictional Discourse" could be said to ground the entire volume, makes these distinctions meaningful—however controversially—when he argues that "whether or not a work is literature is for readers to decide, whether or not it is fictional is for the author to decide.")[53] The essays include Monroe Beardsley's "An Aesthetic Definition of Art" (which argues that "the aesthetic intention . . . must have been present and at least to some degree effective" in its creation of some features of a work);[54] Jerrold Levinson's "What a Musical Work Is" ("instances" of either a "pure" or "indicated" "sound structure" as well as a "structure of performing means specified for realizing the sounds at each point");[55] and Jack W. Meiland's "Originals, Copies, and Aesthetic Value" (which maintains that "there are situations in which aesthetic judgment can be independent of cultural belief").[56] Very little ground separates these conclusions from the assumptions made by our sampling of literary critics. Richard Wollheim's "On Pictorial Representation," included in the anthology for its evaluation of the *experience* of an analytic aesthetics, develops a version of Scarry's "solidity" argument, which he calls "twofoldedness": "Looking at a suitably marked surface, we are visually aware at once of the marked surface and of something in front of or behind something else. . . . one of the pictorial surface, the other of what it represents."[57] This "single experience with two aspects" corresponds to the configuration of a "suitable" piece and the objects it represents, similar to the shadow cast on a wall that draws attention to itself as an instigator of the believability of the wall that it exposes. Clearly, folding together or passing over is supposed to mediate our reception of aesthetic iterations of reference such that we identify them as aesthetic; the philosophy and literary criticism we have been reading recasts that identification as a criterion of the believability, authenticity, and ontology of a work.

I find this conclusion limiting, not because both disciplines wind up retreading old ground—every one of the works I've listed in this introduction is electrifying in the way it thinks the issue through. Rather, it is because the figure directing these approaches—Mill—is a figure that every reference theorist has developed in such a way that his old ground doesn't look the same as it did, and the circumstances that obtain inside of it are vastly more dynamic for retaining their structure. We can keep Mill's propositional form while transposing it onto *sets* of qualities, producing many references to things present, absent, and in-between while suspending and problematizing those categories. Mill's position was that we make assertions about the world by combining names of objects and that the meaning of a nameable object is simply its bearer, a form that could not account for identity statements between co-referring names, sentences containing empty names, negative existentials, and propositional attitude attributions. The theory of reference's struggle to define itself emerges with the question of how to handle these elusive cases. G. E. Moore and Bertrand Russell reacted to the Idealist position that an object is not discrete but exists in virtue of the relations it has (and the references it makes) to other objects; their position was that "propositions" about and "meanings" of objects are structured like ordinary things whose existence is built into our descriptive language. Russell's "realism" about reference expands Millian descriptivism in the sense that it takes up the formal structure of propositions, but it denies that the meaning of entifying references must be contingent on their objects. He agrees that definite descriptions and denoting phrases are incomplete in the Millian sense if they are considered in isolation, and only take on meaning when uttered in a sentence that expresses a proposition, and yet he argues that not all meaningful propositions have to be true. In other words, the mechanism by which an expression refers (its associated descriptive, reference-fixing content) *is* its meaning.[58] This theory, unlike Mill's, has the added benefit of explaining *how* descriptions refer: they refer to their bearers in virtue of the fact that that entity satisfies the descriptions associated with it.

This expanded Millian description theory is the starting point of most subsequent theories of reference, each of which contains the potential to enrich of our understanding of the way novelists handle objects. In Russell's reluctance to take up—in say, the proposition "Pip is shivering"—Mill's position that "shiveringness" is a nameable object (and, we should add, the idea that "Pip" refers at all), he separates references into proper names that denote, demonstrate, and even index objects, and descriptions that are not genuine referring expressions, and denote only through a mediating entity, their descriptive content. It is useful to think of Russell's theory of descriptions in terms of Scarry's theory of solidity, since both turn on a mediation between the thing referenced and the qualities its reference is supposed to express. For Scarry, "solidity" names the connotative quality of a wall that is bound to the wall's being believable—it is equivalent to Millian "shiveringness." For Russell, not so much; the "solidness" of a wall means nothing—rather, "it is only what we may call the *concept* that enters into the proposition," though it contributes to the meaning of a sentence like "the wall is solid," which is always meaningful and sometimes true.[59]

We can direct this question to both Russell and Scarry: By virtue of what is this reference meaningful, believable, or true? P. F. Strawson argues that Russell overlooks the distinction between a sentence and a *use* of a sentence, and that speakers use definite descriptions in order to make statements *about* something, not to verify whether or not it exists; so, depending on the context, "Pip is shivering" refers differently in a class discussion, in a statement about your kid brother, or in a set of stage directions for the school play.[60] Gareth Evans's position takes something from both Russell and Strawson. He argues that thoughts about objects have a bidirectional structure: the thought that "Pip is shivering" would have something in common with the thought that "Magwitch is shivering" and also something in common with the thought that "Pip is sweaty." In all three cases, the references are not made up of different elements but different abilities—in particular, the ability to possess the concept of "shivering." Evans affirms Russell's Principle, that a subject cannot make a judgment about anything unless she knows which object that judgment is about, and argues that to utter the proposition "Pip is shivering" and intend it to be true is to know what it is to be equated with a unique object, and to know what it is to be equated with its property or concept.[61] From Strawson he takes the idea that this knowledge is contextually flexible, that knowledge of what it is for something to be "shivering" can be exercised in indefinitely many distinct thoughts, including its appropriation for Magwitch.

Meanwhile, John Searle argues that there is never only one definite description for any nameable object, but many; also that there is no need for it to be expressed linguistically because speakers carry mental content that is intentionally motivated in their references; and finally that when an object is referenced, that reference isn't in any way the determinative meaning or definition of the object but merely a reference-fixing description that satisfies a momentary communicative need.[62] Saul Kripke believes that we should eliminate descriptive content from nameable objects and also questions of how references carry their own meanings, and instead think of naming as causally oriented in an initial moment when the speaker first learned what something was called, such that every subsequent iteration of the reference must be intended to accord with the originary naming.[63] And Quine and Donald Davidson think that theories of reference are impossible and useless. Quine argues that we need to privilege meaning over reference, because all descriptions have meaning, but reference is inscrutable; there is no reason to invoke reference unless we are talking about some purpose we have in assigning referents to objects.[64] Davidson argues that propositions literally "point out" actual objects in the world, which are their sources, and that there is no mediation at all, no sense data, meanings, or representations that can come between propositions and objects.[65] On this view, our interactions with the world condition whatever representations we have; such a theory is causal in a Kripkean sense, though the reference need not intentionally recall its origin when it is uttered. Another way of describing

Davidson's argument is to say that "the object of the belief (assertion) is a function of the things in the world that normally cause that belief (assertion), *i.e.*, the things in the world that cause it to be *true*."[66]

I've surveyed the breadth of refinements to Mill's propositional form in order to show how useful they could be for our understanding of the way reference works in the novel. Each of these theories tells a story about how we refer. *Object Lessons* combines and reconfigures their positions—in a way, it passes one view over another—not to infuse them with a relevance or animation that to my mind they already have, but to deepen and defamiliarize our view of the way novels, characters, and readers refer to things. References have occasions; they are built of sets of qualities; they are, on the one hand, proper names and, on the other, definite descriptions, and they require different abilities to meet conditions of satisfaction. Why not develop these quirks and capacities, rather than operating from the position that reference negates its objects, abstracts them, embeds them within structures that definitively determine them, or brings them to life and makes them believable, true, or false?

What if Strawson's understanding of descriptions as making propositions were read as and enclosed within propositions themselves, creating a Russellian form that leaks mediations? What if that form were replicated not just in characters' understandings of one another, but used as a device that moves a plot along? These are the questions I ask in chapter 1, on George Meredith's *The Egoist*. What if a novel could be said to dramatize what I've called Searle's theory of the "momentary communicative need," and if the delimitations of that theory—it actually relies on a kind of magical thinking—intervene to keep the novel and its protagonist from some kind of fulfillment? I ask that question in my second chapter, on William Makepeace Thackeray's *Barry Lyndon*. What if a Kripkean reiteratively affirms a mistaken reference, a non-denoting or indefinite description, such that in promising to refer, it succeeds only in referring to itself—in essence, a Quinean's last resort: reference employed to talk about some purpose we have in referring to objects—and how could that produce a correct reference after all? What if such a character's mistakes were echoed in a novel's theory of itself? I ask these questions in my third chapter on Elizabeth Gaskell's novel *Cranford*, a novel that is also attentive to the referential problem of "lost" objects, but rather than tracking them, settles into what philosopher Gareth Evans calls the "fundamental ground of difference" between objects present and absent by mapping them onto a narrative sequence of propositions that can themselves be projectible. The fourth chapter takes up a very human reaction to the power that reference has over our ability to make the world; that the author it deals with is a philosopher makes the point that reference isn't just a philosophical system, but a theory of the novel as well. Iris Murdoch is a Davidsonian, keen to entify descriptions as prompted by objects in the world (both in her fiction and her philosophy); but she is also a lapsed Russellian in her belief that judgments require subjects in view of a unique x. This leads her to the conclusion that if our judgments of objects—and people as objects—are bound to an epistemological knowledge of what they are like, and if those judgments directly engage things in the world that have the capacity to hurt us, it's best to think of them as kindly as possible.

1

Meredith & Ends

A *description* is composed of sentences whose order one can generally *reverse*: I can describe this room by a series of clauses whose order is not important. A gaze roams as it wishes. Nothing more natural, nothing more *true*, than this vagrancy; for . . . *truth is chance.*

But, if this latitude, and the habit of facility which goes with it, become the dominating factor, it gradually dissuades writers from employing their ability for abstraction, just as it reduces to nothing the slightest necessity for concentration on the reader's part, in order *to win him over with immediate effects*, rhetorical shock tactics . . .

This mode of creating, legitimate in principle, and to which we owe so many beautiful things, leads, like the abuse of landscape, *to the diminution of the intellectual part of art.*

« PAUL VALÉRY, "Degas, Danse, Dessin" »

George Meredith is a canonical writer generally agreed to be bad at writing, and this chapter is less about why this is the case or how one could go about recovering him, than it is about what we find in Meredith when we are no longer looking. I will complicate the assumption, adapted from Valéry above, that novelists share a fraught relationship to the work that description does; that the task of the novelist is to motivate character, plot, and "intellect" in spite of it; and that the result separates good novels from bad. There is a grandeur in the simplicity of my approach that smacks of Meredith—he opens his 1879 novel *The Egoist* by pitting The Comic Spirit against The Book of Earth—but I intend to make use of a kind of modest close reading that is in many ways counterintuitive to the way we read novels in general and Meredith in particular. Rather than seizing on his attempts at motivated description in order to accumulate conflicting or corroborating interpretations of why he's saying what he says the way he says it, I want to isolate and reduce the semantic content of those descriptions to the point where they mean very little. This will allow me to resituate the trade-off that Valéry describes between the detail and the abstraction, so that, rather than engaging arguments about the reflexive complexity of the novel genre and its contemporary social or "intellectual" commitments, I can create a harmonics between Meredith's granular descriptions and the philosophy of language. This discourse, concerned with *how* words mean but not what or why, will offer us a different approach to the mechanics of description, and a new vocabulary for its role in novel theory.

The first page of the *Critical Heritage* anthology devoted to Meredith's reception levels its attack at his "difficult" style, "liable to charges of affectation, obscurity, structural weakness, and a lack of proportion." Even worse, his bad descriptions are contagious: it is, it seems, impossible for critics to distinguish between them, for they often use the same examples to evidence "his successful experiments and his lapses from good taste." There has never been agreement "about his permanent place in letters," and arguments to this effect abound in "bitterness and exaggeration." Even in his own lifetime, when one is often valued just for hanging on, Meredith "failed to make an impact on the public at large or to obtain from the critical Press the degree of respect and understanding to which he was entitled."[1] This is grim stuff, but it is charged with the inducement of a dare; Meredith's awfulness is just an obstacle to be overcome, and our resistance to his intricacy is born of both an unimaginative relationship to the pleasures of description, and an unrigorous examination of the reasons why we read what we do.

Meredith's "lapses in good taste," figured as "affectation" and "obscurity" in the *Critical Heritage*, galvanize the distinction Valéry makes between the chanciness of particularity and the stability of abstraction, and recast his separation of description from the "intellectual part of art" as a *process*, a syllogism that folds Meredith's abstractions into his accretion of details.[2] Critics have tried to account for this rhetorical process by turning to the compression of his aphorisms. In "The Decay of Lying" Oscar Wilde writes that Meredith "is always breaking his shins over his own wit" and that "By its means he has planted round his garden a hedge full of thorns, and red with wonderful roses."[3] Something in those roses stands in for both Meredith's aestheticism *and* its origins; his martyrdom makes itself reiteratively available as an act and its product, so that in ignoring his critics and hurting himself, he produces a thing of beauty that none but the most discriminating reader can see, and then can only reference as an exquisite *act*. Wilde shows us how much easier it is to explain this effect than its cause. His evaluation is less about describing what isn't there than in referencing something that isn't describable; he effectively reenacts the postponements, refractions, and otherwise subtended complications of Meredith's project even while holding them dear. In taking what Meredith does for what Meredith is, Wilde conveys Meredith's badness through a conceptual displacement that substitutes the method for the work itself. Meredith falls from the useful, the beautiful, and the good—his taste is only *lapsed*—and the less that remains is an invitation to explicate him.[4]

What Wilde is reaching for is a sliding between two incommensurable terms: Meredith's particulars and his universals, his difficultly and his ease, his style and his subject. He is reaching, in other words, for an *accommodation* for the reader, a relation that would both name the space between and hold still the way back and forth between one term and another. Throughout this chapter, I will be assuming two commonsense behaviors that accommodation entails: first, that in any conversation between Meredith and his readers, the readers assume certain information in order for that conversation to make sense, in order to accommodate themselves to Meredith's way of thinking; and second, that readers who cannot reasonably accommodate themselves to Meredith's way of thinking begin to shift their assumptions, destabilizing their position in relation to Meredith and the assumptions that lie behind that position. In other words, accommodation understands Meredith's descriptions to be inseparable from their eventual interpretation; it marks the capacity to conceptualize one thing in and through another, but what results from that conceptualization is always going to be an unfounded guess.[5]

This chapter is an attempt to put some pressure on this series of displacements, arguing throughout that what we have seen in the criticism of Meredith's work is an unfinished and misleading version of the work he is doing in his fiction. Rather than looking at the static *images* that he describes as isolatable and inherently meaningless—his accretive metaphors, aphorisms, and characterizations—I will draw on their use in Meredith's descriptions of postponed or incomplete *action*. I will stick with *The Egoist*, the novel that the summary judgment of the *Critical Heritage* considers his most characteristic (and characteristically irritating), and I will argue that what we think of as the displacements in Meredith's descriptions are actually crucial sources of motivation in themselves, for both his novel's structure and plot, and his intellectual project as a whole. This approach explicitly counters those critical gestures that attach descriptions to their own interpretative unpacking, because I think Meredith's descriptions contain and embody their own interpretations, just as any other performed action could be said to contain the intentions that caused it to happen. I have chosen to analyze descriptions of intentional action because they encourage a reader's interpretation; I choose descriptions of intentional action in Meredith's work because his aphoristic tendencies point to a mind interested in the way meaning is conveyed; and I choose such descriptions because novels are about action, and embedding meaning in actions is always going to be tricky for an aphorist.

One of the more consistent assumptions of critics who deal with the intentional structure of a text is that the designers of a text are by definition the actors whose conception of a thing determines *how it is*, and *how it is* is an expressive capacity that cannot be understood apart from a participation in its sociolinguistic practices. To say this several different ways: an author's intention is present-tense representation; it is a potentially knowledge-bearing state that generates the facts that make it true; it is productive of what is already known, and it realizes the author's knowledge of it. In this vein, Steven Knapp and Walter Benn Michaels have argued that there can be no *intentionless* meanings,[6] and Wimsatt and Beardsley claim that "[j]udging a poem is like judging a pudding or a machine" in that only if it "works" at all do we infer the intention of its artificer.[7] Even Paul de Man and Michel Foucault, while explicitly refuting this evaluative characterization of literature as an intentional action, cannot help but slide into an hermeneutical dead-end when discussing it: de Man argues that "interpretation of an intentional act or an intentional object always implies an *understanding* of the intent,"[8] and Foucault argues that despite the irrelevance of the interiority of intentions, thoughts, or subjects, their (seemingly inevitable) dispersion as an exteriority is rooted "in the search for totalities, the descriptions of relations of exteriority for the theme of the transcendental foundation, [and] the analysis of accumulations for the quest of the origin."[9] This trajectory, from the New Critical insistence on the explication of the autonomous text to a deconstructive insistence on the system of relations that circumscribe both reader and text into a kind of mutual deterritorialization, displaces the irreducible *particularity* of intentional descriptions, actions, and descriptions-of-actions. In applying coherence to potentially isolatable and inherently meaningless things, it reenacts the slide from the object to its interpretation in the same way that Meredith's critics have, embedding the thing done into its doing.

This chapter takes the opposite position: that objects like described intentional actions—especially when atomized in and as aphoristic images—entail their interpretations as processes *internal to themselves*. In being isolatable, they are not meaningless; their reference to a specific act is not constitutive of their meaning. Rather, their compression creates a friction whose meaning self-presents. When we follow this track to its conclusion, our definition of intention changes. We begin to think of descriptions as essences that express a *process* of understanding intention as an analysis of the links between the details that make an action intentional. Ludwig Wittgenstein makes this point:

> "I was going to say. . . ."—You remember various details. But not even all of them together shew your intention. It is as if a snapshot of a scene had been taken, but only a few scattered details of it were to be seen: here a hand, there a bit of face, or a hat—the rest is dark. And now it is as if we knew quite certainly what the whole picture represented. As if I could read the darkness.
>
> These "details" are not irrelevant in the sense in which other circumstances which I can remember equally well are irrelevant. But if I tell someone "For a moment I was going to say, . . ." he does not learn those details from this, nor need he guess them. He need not know, for instance, that I had already opened my mouth to speak. But he *can* "fill out the picture" in this way. (And this capacity is part of understanding what I tell him.)[10]

The easiest way of thinking about the kinds of connections Wittgenstein considers crucial to "filling in" the picture of an intentional action is to look at the scene itself and not at the story behind it. We should be prepared to read the darkness, to allow ourselves not to account for everything or to situate it inside a wider, more empirical understanding of the way we rationalize and narrativize action; rather, we should intuitively sense the *noncalculative* reasons behind intentional action. Philosopher Candace Vogler gives us the simple act of crossing a street: "You shift weight to one foot *and* step off the curb *and* step onto the street *and* enter the café at the other side. This is true and, we may suppose, what you intend. What we cannot say is that you *A*, *B*, and *C* in order to cross the road, or that you cross the road in order to get to the other side, or that you intend anything that might be expressed in this idiom."[11] Like the assumption that Wittgenstein had "opened his mouth to speak" without having to say it, the movement from one foot to the other is filled in with a practical consideration, not a consideration of desirability. "And the best that I can propose" Wittgenstein writes, "is that we should yield to the temptation to use this picture, but then investigate how the *application* of the picture goes."[12] Practical considerations make the person acting king of whatever logical end the action fills in, but it is the process of *determining* that logical end from the scant components of a composite picture in the darkness that pressurizes and expresses the description it evokes. So, some descriptions of walking across the street will be true, but not others, and the ones that can be excluded are excluded because they involve predictions about ends other than the ones inside the edges of the snapshot.

We can see from Wittgenstein's interpretation that isolating descriptions of intentional action can generate a different kind of meaning from that which we get when we overload objects with a presumptive analysis of the epistemologies that will disclose their intention. In the aphoristic terms that are shot through both Meredith's and Wittgenstein's prose, *describing is witnessing*. "Don't think but look!"[13] The snapshot discloses forms of propositions that are independent of what can be experienced empirically, psychologically, and speculatively. Thus, the question we ought to ask of the literary criticism of descriptions is, "Does it contain any ontological, metaphysical, religious, or epistemological presupposition?" If it does, it cannot properly account for the structural aspects of our understanding.[14] The pressure inside a description is caused by the heaping up of isolated details that are frustrated by their present-ness, their inability to gesture or develop outward; they can only evoke resemblances, echoes, and relations. The question for analytic philosophy, then, is not "What is the snapshot a snapshot *of*?" but "How do we use statements to express our sudden *understanding* of the snapshot?"—the statements that produce Wittgenstein's admittedly optimistic effect: "And now it is as if we knew quite certainly what the whole picture represented." We are not scrutinizing an inner psychological experience that guides our understanding, but the actual use we make of it; by reference to its obtaining circumstances, the structure of language reveals the structure of "what is."

I have arranged the remainder of this chapter into three parts: first, I concentrate on Meredith's descriptions at the level of the sentence, reading a moment in *The Egoist* that analytic philosophy can illuminate as crucial for an understanding of the relation between characterization and description in Meredith's work. Second, I explain the ways in which the density of these descriptions creates characters through their intentional actions in the novel. Finally, I demonstrate, using significant moments of descriptive activity in *The Egoist*, how an analytic philosophy of action could reveal new sources of motivation in the broader organization of this novel and in others. Scenes that are considered unproductive in terms of the movement of the novel's plot and character development, moments that show us Meredith at what has seemed like his least disciplined, are reintegrated into a broader understanding of his project and its repudiation of the kinds of displacements and gestures outward—displacements that I have termed accommodations—that we have found in his critical heritage and the criticism of literary description in general. I hope to show that the "failure" that critics apologize for entails a far more productive understanding of narration and its engines; rather than saying so very much, we will find Meredith saying as precious little as possible about problems that have yet to receive the description they deserve.

As Meredith's *The Egoist* begins, Sir Willoughby Patterne is described as enjoying the *proposition* of proposing to Clara Middleton; he enjoys *the fact that* "she had money and health and beauty, the triune of perfect starriness, which makes all men astronomers."[15] Clara, however, enjoys *the fact that* Willoughby *flaunts* his "amiable superlatives" in front of her: "He was the heir of successful competitors. He had a style, a tone, an artist tailor, an authority of manner: he had in the hopeful ardour of the chase among a multitude a freshness that gave him advantage; and together with his undeviating energy when there was a prize to be won and possessed, these were scarcely resistible. He spared no pains, for he was adust and athirst for the winning-post" (*E*, 33). Enjoyment, for Meredith's lovers, is a verb that becomes connected to a predicate in unusual, contradictory ways. G. E. M. Anscombe, one of analytic philosophy's most prominent practitioners, a protégé and translator of Wittgenstein, and a formidable interrogator of the emotional language we use to describe intentional descriptions, shows us how this happens. In her 1967 analysis of the predicative connection between the language of emotion and its object, "On the Grammar of 'Enjoy,'" she argues that though speakers of conventional English are often tempted to think of the verb *to enjoy* as being able to take both an object and a proposition—for example, "I enjoyed *X*-ing," and "I enjoyed *the fact that* I was *X*-ing"—the idea of enjoying a proposition is ridiculous unless we think of the proposition as being predicatively connected to the verb *enjoy* through a further expression crucial to the understanding of the verb's object.[16] So, if at a party like the one that occasions Willoughby's introduction to Clara, "I enjoyed talking to the most handsome person present," then the fact that this person is handsome is predicatively connected to my enjoyment of our conversation. I do not enjoy talking to a person who just *happens* to be the most handsome one there; rather, I enjoyed talking to her *because* of this handsomeness.[17] Willoughby is interested in the fact of Clara's having the "triune of perfect starriness" rather than enjoying her money, enjoying her health, and enjoying her beauty in themselves. The whole that these things make in the form of a proposition about Clara, at once and together, is more enjoyable for Willoughby than the sum of its parts.

We are thus introduced to our egoist through his odd substitution of a proposition for Clara herself, an enjoyment of factors that do not, in themselves or even together, produce sufficient enjoyment. The description of Clara's own enjoyment involves a similar abstraction, but locates it in the fact of Willoughby's *presentation* of his advantages. It is not simply that he produces the effect of superlatives held in combination, but that he presents them to her with ardor and competitiveness. Thus, the descriptions that characterize Clara's interest in Willoughby allow her to be read as comparatively more "human" than he is because they are connected to the *effort* he makes to present them. The characterological force of their meeting, the thing that makes Clara more sympathetic and consequently more interesting to readers than Willoughby, is her move from an enjoyment of an abstraction (an enjoyment of the fact of "having") to an enjoyment of the *generation* of an abstraction (an enjoyment of the fact of "showing" to have). Both the descriptions of the relation between Clara's enjoyment and Willoughby's and Meredith's style and content thus share a stake in intentional action—they try to make sense of behavior through an analysis of the way that behavior is described—and return us from that analysis of intentional action back to its place within the form of *The Egoist* as a whole.

What this shared tendency illustrates to us, I think, is that the naming of an intentional action in Meredith is productively evocative of its content without ever being interested in specifically denoting that content. Characters are valued for the descriptions that they inspire in others instead of the presence or absence of their interiority; descriptions stack up accretively without evolving, aiming for impaction rather than accuracy, and the plot that encloses them maintains an intentional form while retaining none of its narratives.[18] The sheer number of these lonely complexities draws our attention to the value and motivation inherent in the description of intentional actions. We come to feel their value as the experience of their impaction, and are made aware of all the ways that their isolation generates content. Therefore, to understand *The Egoist*, and perhaps all novels, is to understand the way that an author's response to accommodation—to the relation between details and their interpretations—brings critical attention to the novel's own reliance on the description of intentional actions. In this instance, Meredith is refusing accommodation in two ways: when Willoughby enjoys

Clara's attributes, he comes up with the fact that they exist but not the process involved in enjoying them, and when Clara enjoys the way Willoughby presents the fact of his attributes, she is not enjoying the attributes themselves. Both approaches short-circuit the slide from details to their interpretations, and say a great deal—almost immediately—about Meredith's stake in the mechanics of description.

Meredith's preface to *The Egoist* so effortlessly tempts us into connecting details and their interpretations that it is easy to see how we have missed their fragmentation. Meredith is said to so enclose all characters within himself and his proxy narrators that they become facets of a single personality; they share thoughts that are similarly complex, exist within a hermetically sealed timespace, and are effortlessly substitutional, leaving the novel only on the condition that other characters take their places. The central tenet of the preface is an aphoristic version of this system: "Comedy is a game played to throw reflections upon social life, and it deals with human nature in the drawing-room of civilized men and women, where we have no dust of the struggling outer world, no mire, no violent crashes, to make the correctness of the representation convincing. Credulity is not wooed through the impressionable senses; nor have we recourse to the small circular glow of the watchmaker's eye to raise in bright relief minutest grains of evidence for the routing of incredulity" (*E*, 3).

Here, Meredith suspends us between the convincing representation of social life and its rarefied referentiality in fiction. Credulity lies in ideas themselves, a happy coincidence for the writer who has no intention of recording the detached and irrelevant influences of the world outside the mind. Whatever representations exist in Meredith's novels will know themselves to be self-referential and incomplete; they are integrated within the text as localized gestures, detached from the kinds of contextualizing interpretations that his readers are always trying to perform. If we look at the characterization of activity that will *not* be included in Meredith's approach—the dust of the struggling outer world, the violent crashes, the mire—and see it connected to the verb *to make*, as in, "to make the correctness of the representation convincing," we notice that the object of the verb is propositional. The *fact* that the world is comprised of a series of despairingly incoherent, leaky accidents, uninterrupted by moments of reliable coherence, means that they could turn the form of comedy into something else. The entire plot of *The Egoist* hangs on its heroine's dawning realization of her entrapment at a country house; the "struggling outer world" pressurizes the text, but it is never explicitly mentioned or described. Meredith uses the verb *to make* here to stand in for what description will do in the absence of that "outer world," illuminating for us the extent to which he sees description as a crucial site of formal structuration. Without an extremely constricted theory of description that converts all depictions of character motivation, intention, and action into compressed isolation, his text could be destabilized, co-implicating both its form and its genre into a meaningless agglutination.

In *George Meredith and English Comedy*, V. S. Pritchett argues that the containment of Meredith's descriptions begs for the reader's projection into the text and out again: "Meredith thought of images, whether lyrical or comic, as promoters of dramatic movement. They are meant to give energy. The mind is made to give a leap into fantasy and, with it, the scene is agitated."[19] "Meant," like "made," reads as an apology for Meredith's squandering investment in all images as movement, but Pritchett's explanation neglects the most important process: that by which the reader actively agitates the scene. How does our leap through image produce action? Is there a corroborating effect that guarantees our interpretation of that image, or is the variable not just the image's genre, "whether lyrical or comic," but the potential misinterpretations that any one image would carry?

Pritchett chalks up Meredith's failure to energize his images to the sheer number of them and gives us an oft-quoted passage from his 1895 novel *The Amazing Marriage*, "a passage that upset Edmund Gosse," describing a gambling table:

> He compared the creatures dabbling over the board to summer flies on butcher's meat, periodically scared by a cloth. More in the ab-

stract they were snatching at a snapdragon bowl. It struck him that the gamblers had thronged in an invitation to drink the round of seed time and harvest at one gulp. Again they were desperate gleaners, hopping, skipping, bleeding, amid a whiz of scythe-blades, for small wisps of booty. Nor was it long before the presidency of an ancient hoary Goat-Satan might be perceived, with skew-eyes, nursing a hoof on a tree.[20]

"Four attempts to find a metaphor for gambling when one is required," Pritchett writes, "[a]nd they are all—unless in the mind of a farmer—inapt."[21] The viscosity of this passage, its gleaning, snapdragons, and butcher's meat, effects a tepid equilibrium, stopping the action cold and presenting us with little more than a writerly exercise, where "the only good image . . . is 'the skew-eye of the goat'"—which still isn't worth the leap. Meredith uses metonymic comparatives as a narrative engine, relating meat to a bowl of snapdragons—an "abstraction" afforded by its simplicity, since a bowl is easier to imagine than the randomness of flies—and then "strikes" his description home as a compromise between the two, the sporadic and the solid becoming seeding and harvest, and then the "gleaners" at last an uncharacterized vapor, preying on and preyed upon at once. The Goat-Satan that contracts these descriptions to their various roles—the personification of Meredith's own punishingly bad efforts at imagery and thus the implicit pun on *scapegoat*—quite simply has to be the most present description in the piece, as it anchors and explains the "hoary" rest. Thus, what Pritchett claims of Meredith's other descriptions particularly fails this one. Our "leap into fantasy" works to harmonize a scene if the images are impacted in the way we've discussed, but any effort to put this series into action gives us the "mind of a farmer."

The character in question, Gower Woodseer, is introduced in a chapter entitled "The Natural Philosopher" in an attitude remarkably similar to that of our Goat-Satan ("nursing a bruised leg, not in the easiest of postures, on a sharp tooth of rock"),[22] so Pritchett must be objecting to something larger in this passage. If the difficulty lies less in the *kind* of images Meredith is describing than in the sheer *amount* of them, and if, although Pritchett knows Woodseer to be a naturalist, these images are "inapt" unless in the mind of a "farmer," we can only make sense of his objection in terms of a lack of *movement* in the images, a sense in which they are inadequate to the task because individually they express more about their origin than the object they're describing, and their origin is too flatly described. They lack accommodation, stack up without developing, and point neither to gambling nor to Woodseer himself with sufficient depth.[23] We are invited to enjoy both these images and the plot that contains them in the same way that Willoughby at first enjoyed Clara: as a complex proposition charged with an energy that derives not from the quality of one thing or another but from the fact of their extreme Meredithean impaction. We like them not because of what they are—we cannot say just what they are—but because of all there is to say about them.

Meredith's approach to language is about its use: the way we, as readers and speakers, exercise discrete semantic rules in our understanding of description. A reader demonstrates her mastery of a language through her ability to make and comprehend sentences of that language, including an indefinite many that are wholly novel to her. This is possible, Meredith demonstrates, by bundling together enough cues that a reader can take in all of their variants at once. Look at the temporal organization of the gambling passage: Woodseer compares the creatures and then reconceptualizes them "more in the abstract," and then "again." We haven't suspensions, or displacements, or accretions at all, but a temporal sequence separating each description at different levels of abstraction. They cannot be compared from either direction, nor can we think of them as revisions of one another, erasing the one that came before, because the conjunctive structure of the sentence embeds each description into its own referential system. Like the plot of *The Egoist*, pressurized from without by the "mire" of the world beyond it, Meredith's descriptions in this passage and others are both condensed and agitated, invoking the kinds of active-use semantic rules that charge isolated images with meaning.

Chapter 13 is conspicuously titled "The First Effort After Freedom," and promises something like the first real action of a novel in which nothing much happens. Clara has engaged herself to Willoughby and is spending an indeterminate amount of time living on his estate with her father before the wedding. She has become increasingly certain that her engagement is a mistake, and after a lively dinner with Laetitia Dale, the neighboring spinster who has pined for Willoughby for years and is a much better match—not least because her interest in him makes her susceptible to the suggestion—Clara decides to convince Willoughby that Laetitia's is a truer love and free herself by a substitution. Thus the first effort *after* freedom does bidirectional work here: Clara's confrontation is a both a means to the end of freedom, and her first real shove at Willoughby since their engagement.

Clara's inspired recognition of this space between freedoms follows her introduction to Willoughby's cousin Vernon Whitford, who will emerge as her love interest and escape clause at the novel's close, and whose impression of stability, intelligence, and vigor throws what she determines to be Willoughby's "nonsensical," "incomprehensible" egoism, the "something illogical in him" into relief:

> She resolved that she would one day, one distant day provoke it—upon what? The special point eluded her. . . . That 'something illogical' had stirred her feelings more than her intellect to revolt. She could not constitute herself the advocate of Mr. Whitford. Still she marked the disputation for an event to come.
>
> Meditating on it, she fell to picturing Sir Willoughby's face at the first accents of his bride's decided disagreement with him. The picture once conjured up would not be laid. He was handsome; so correctly handsome, that a slight unfriendly touch precipitated him into caricature. His habitual air of happy pride, of indignant contentment rather, could easily be overdone. Surprise, when he threw emphasis on it, stretched him with the tall eyebrows of a mask—limitless under the spell of caricature; and in time, whenever she was

not pleased by her thoughts, she had that, and not his likeness, for the vision of him. (*E*, 41)

The passage is worth quoting at length for the questions it raises and ducks; Clara has resolved to end things but doesn't know when or why, the scene's to-be-announcedness invoking little more than a curiosity to see the look on Willoughby's face. As a mask with infinite eyebrows stretches him up and away, she lets a "something illogical" overtake him in the shared sense of the word "precipitate," a "slight unfriendly touch" that both hurries him into caricature, and leaves caricature remaining in deposit after all of its containment has burned off. There is a "hurry up and wait" paradox about Meredith's phrasing here, suggesting that caricature—already both surface and core—is the material dissolve of the similarly impacted "happy pride" and "indignant contentment." The "slight unfriendly touch" that destabilizes those two states—each already impacted as a contradiction—is destabilizing something fortified and compressed, a space beyond plans and immune to suggestion. The state of being happy, proud, indignant, or content is actionless, so the conflicted pairing looks counterfactual and foreclosed.[24]

This is a separation between plot and character engaged at a cellular level, where Willoughby's self-realizing states are co-opted by Clara's other evolving descriptions. There would be no motivation for Willoughby to leave a place of "indignant contentment," but because this place doubles as Clara's motivation for some form of intentional action, it becomes temporary and vulnerable. Additionally, the narrative that drives her agenda has no end; Clara is "resolved" in a way that couldn't be called calculative, given her unexpected (and temporarily satisfying) fixation on Willoughby's face. There is an ethical argument in the precipitate, as pride and indignation are codified vices for Meredith and bring a sense of injustice to bear on Willoughby's ease. When Clara amplifies his look, however, it's clear that she doesn't see its immorality so much as its disturbance. Our attempts to connect

Meredith's descriptions to one another break down at every point, since they not only self-fortify in the face of the characters who conjure but cannot control them, but also emphasize their significance by reappearing every time their objects are referenced. Meredith is saying as little as possible about both of these characters, but their descriptions are pressurized and evocative.

Clara's catalyzing event-to-come is intended to unseat Willoughby, but his "something illogical" and various paradoxes characterize him as already unstable, a stacked abundance of imagery that leads to an oversimplification. Clara will "one day, one distant day" provoke Willoughby, and he is "handsome; so correctly handsome." Both modifiers make a point of adding nothing to the phrases that exist without them, instead specifying a particular kind of vagueness. Clara "marked the disputation for an event to come," what will be called "his bride's decided disagreement with him," two descriptions that but passively implicate her, refusing to locate their object in anything other than an abstraction. Here again we have the excesses of "decided" and "marked," the first an emphasis that actually conflicts with "disagreement," and the second a notation that is without significance, but which the predicate "an event to come" enacts. Lastly, Clara "fell to picturing" Willoughby's face, the picture "once conjured up would not be laid," and "in time . . . she had that, and not his likeness, for the vision of him," three ways of describing a daydream as both a doing and a thing done, a raising and a falling down—actions that don't contradict one another so much as reposition Clara as a victim of her own imagination.

The movement into abstraction that we get with the dissociation of "his bride's disagreement" is acting this out for us, as indicated by the supernatural tinge of the "conjured" "spell of caricature" that "would not be laid." The lines that describe the mask *behave* it, as if the description itself becomes Willoughby's "something illogical": "And it was unjust, contrary to her deeper feelings; she rebuked herself, and as much as her naughty spirit permitted, she tried to look on him as the world did; an effort inducing reflections upon the blessings of ignorance. She seemed to herself beset by a circle of imps, hardly responsible for her thoughts" (*E*, 41–42). Thus, the descriptions of intentional action that reinscribe Willoughby's and Clara's positions within the novel also give us a sense of its conjuring agency, and show us just how arbitrary some of Clara's grounds for acting might seem. This will complicate our reception of the novel's plot, not simply because scenes like this underscore Clara's lack of a deliberative process, but because they show her *trying* to have one. Clara is incapable of dismissing the caricature that she has invented, il- luminating a gap between her experience of an action and the in- tentional descriptions that Meredith uses to mobilize the novel.

Meredith is modeling decision-making in a rigorously self- conscious way that shows us how the intention in the agent is likewise in the act: Clara tries to imagine an action and its con- sequences, only to find that her central description takes over, enclosing the entire action within itself, fortifying its borders with the hard and oversimplifying outline of a caricature, and substituting itself for infinite Willoughbys, the object of the verb. Anscombe's "grammar" of enjoyment supports Clara's experience of her caricature by arguing that our descriptions of intentional action are contingent not on our absolute knowledge of what we are doing, since we can be ignorant of our objectives, their consequences, and of many of the descriptions true of the ac- tion we are performing, but instead on what descriptions can be shown to be relevant to an understanding of the ends for which the action is performed and to the practical considerations we have for thinking that what we are doing contributes to their attainment. Clara's description, though it begins as an enjoyably nasty fantasy of revenge, configures the mask of Willoughby's face as a product of compression, completely walled off from the influence that initiates and pressurizes it and yet activated by its own internal meaning. *These* are the ends of Clara's interpreta- tion: she doesn't need to engage in accommodation to make her object comprehensive and intelligible. It is what it is, and it is intractably, scarily alive.

We have seen Willoughby and Clara diverge in their enjoyment of propositions, and their reactions to one another's descriptions of those propositions, but as the novel progresses, their divergences become much more pronounced. Threatened by her lack of enthusiasm, Willoughby tries to convince Clara of the sacredness of their engagement by describing it as a quirky kind of path: "I am, we will say, riding home from the hunt: I see you awaiting me: I read your heart as though you were beside me. And I know I am coming to the one who reads mine!" (*E*, 53). "Home from the hunt" is a bifocal image, an end beyond an end *and* a destination that Willoughby carries with him, "as though you were beside me." His new ideal is a "we will say," a sustaining place of meaning that describes action while it emerges as an accompaniment to and a place beyond action's ends; were we to do a little arithmetic, we could see the simultaneity of these two sustaining places "adding up" to a single description of intentional action.

It is flatly unsatisfying to assume that Willoughby is careless, or overly careful, in his choice of descriptions because he is responding to Clara's indifference. But his description, elliptical and weird, gives us only the sparest sense of the characterization behind it, and returns us to language when we are most encouraged to make sense of its motivating psychology.[25] When Anscombe writes about the way we understand the ends of our actions and the practical considerations leading to their attainment—the "intentional" part of intentional action—she returns to the idea of the enjoyment of the proposition and refits "the fact that" as our "grounds" for acting. "Grounds" are not reasons "suggesting what is probable, or likely to happen"; instead, they are reasons "suggesting what it would be good to make happen with a view to an objective."[26] Grounds show what good the action is. And like propositions, grounds exist in descriptions of what one is doing in language, not in internal psychological states. Anscombe is saying that in life, we understand an actor's intention when our descriptions of what she is doing seem accurate to her, when she can see the connection between that description, her own ends, and the reasons she has for thinking that what she is doing will bring those ends about. This is as close as we can get to the mental causes of action in analytic philosophy—that is, not very close—but in *The Egoist*, or in any novel, we can only unpack an *order*, the *form* of an intentional action sequence. "Grounds" are in the act, so the description of the act serves as both the form that the action has taken and the grounds that drive it forward. If we are told that Willoughby knew he was riding home from the hunt but didn't know he was riding to a home that had burned down, then under the first description we would read his action as intentional, but under the second, we would not.[27]

Given Willoughby's attraction to the "home from the hunt" image as a description of the constant, isolating present-ness of love, it is unsurprising that the "world" outside will soon become the "principal topic of dissension" between him and Clara. Meredith will use their descriptions of "the world" to expand on their very different perspectives, but rather than leaving Clara and Willoughby trenchantly opposed, he will show us how the structure and evocation of their descriptions can be both separate and simultaneous:

> He explained to his darling that lovers of necessity do loathe the world. They live in the world, they accept its benefits, and assist it as well as they can. In their hearts they must despise it, shut it out, that their love for one another may pour in a clear channel, and with all the force they have. . . .
>
> She shook her head; she could not see it. She would admit none of the notorious errors of the world; its back-biting, selfishness, coarseness, intrusiveness, infectiousness. . . . She spoilt the secret bowersong he delighted to tell over to her. And how, Powers of Love! is love-making to be pursued if we may not kick the world out of our bower and wash our hands of it? Love that does not spurn the world when lovers curtain themselves is a love—is it not so?—that seems to the unwhipped scoffing world to go slinking into basiation's obscurity, instead of on a glorious march behind the screen. (*E*, 40)

This description shows us Willoughby's subjectivity emerging through a reading of Clara's disagreement—that is, without the reciprocal understanding of his own position that would make the knowledge a "thinking with" Clara rather than, say, a "thinking about" her. This disjunction is the product of a strangely bivalent description of intentional action; the screen that separates lovers from the world can shield "basiation's obscurity" *or* project their "glorious march" outward, depending on their delivery through it. The manner in which lovers leave the world to pursue their private rituals leaves on the screen that separates them from that world the residue of whatever intention they take behind it. The description of reciprocal knowledge that constitutes Clara and Willoughby as a couple is subject to intentions that are most legible at the moment she and Willoughby "become" alone.

Theirs is a misunderstanding of the description of the screen between public and private; Willoughby "knew it to be the world which must furnish the dry sticks for the bonfire of a woman's worship," and thus needed it somewhere in his description, but Clara "would not burn the world for him . . . [would not] reduce herself to ashes, or incense, or essence, in honour of him, and so, by love's transmutation, literally be the man she was to marry" (*E*, 41). Clara envisions an inferno burning everything at the altar of Willoughby's ego, while he sees the world hovering up in front of them as she rejects it in his favor, its fine opinion of him lingering as a testament to her choice. By constituting Willoughby *as* the screen, Clara aligns him with his description, their love a "glorified march" into one another. But in order for her to be capable of his reification, some distinction must be made between her and the rest of the world. Unlike Clara's sublime self-alienation in front of the caricature she builds and loses control over, Willoughby describes himself as making something for her to share with him; instead of losing control over the thing he is describing, Willoughby loses control over the thing he describes in the process of describing it to someone else. The accommodation that slides details into their interpretation is once again flummoxed by an attempt to make meaning narratively communicable. In this way, Meredith accords Willoughby's version an unexpected pathos; the way he takes up Clara's objections, frustrated that she "could not see" what he is making for her, paints a sympathetic portrait of descriptions as an understanding of another person as an object in the darkness, surrounded by an unbridgeable gap.

The disagreement between Clara and Willoughby over the meaning of the screen stages the fundamental difficulty Meredith has with descriptions of intentional action and prepares us for the way he will work through them as *The Egoist* develops. Meredith is repeating the very structure that introduced us to Clara and Willoughby at the beginning of the novel: she made the gradual slide from enjoying a proposition to enjoying the building of a proposition, which led her to enjoy the builder; here she hates it, and him. Willoughby enjoyed the proposition, which made natural the slide from Clara to the loving of her; here that slide is destructive. She is incapable of seeing *how* Willoughby is meaning what he says, and he is incapable of seeing *what* she sees. This is the way Meredith "builds" his characters out of their reactions to descriptions of intentional actions: their consistent interpretative processes produce different readings in different contexts, and the fact that we feel that these different contexts *should* contain descriptions of the problems the characters face *and* descriptions of their solutions to these problems pressurizes every one of these contexts into a self-sustaining intentional action whose content is unclear. In other words, what reading for their interpretative processes does to this moment in the text is highlight the fact that Clara and Willoughby miss the description of the *screen* as a *snapshot*—in this case, of Willoughby's intention—that says, quite simply, *here is the thing I am saying*. The fact that Willoughby builds this for Clara is all we are supposed to know; its looming qualities are the action inside of it, the pressurized descriptions of what he intends.

If we rethink intentionality as a thing one moves with and toward, we recast the description of intentional action as the person one is when one is intending, defining character in and through plot. Meredith is going to show us that the irreducibility of the screen on which so much depends does not imply that there is no "there" there, but that it is a description we can find working at many different levels of meaning in the text. Thus, what we have seen in Meredith's sentences and in his characters, we will see in his plotting. Willoughby will try repeatedly to repair the relationship that is always slipping away, and Clara will try to build a proposition whose building aligns with its builder. In the final section of this paper, I show the enactment and effect of these reiterations in the text, and illuminate the ways they enforce the aphoristic isolation of descriptions of intentional actions in the novel form as a whole.

The problem Meredith stages between Willoughby and Clara is derived from their inability to unpack a description to similar ends. Their ways of describing each other and each other's intentions originate in their opposed enjoyments of propositions, and as the structure and content of their arguments become increasingly replicable throughout the novel, Clara and Willoughby themselves become less particularized. All that remains of them are the encrusted aphorisms they throw at each other, so they become abstracted into the positions they held, their arguments evacuated of content. In the last chapters of *The Egoist*, Meredith backs off of the darkness between Willoughby and Clara. He searches for a description of the moment when Willoughby looks for just the right image to describe his intentions to her and the moment when she resists the building of that description. Meredith wants to know what that moment looks like, the moment when one position isolates itself in relation to another, and how it could take us to a greater understanding of the power of description in our readings of other people, their actions, and by extension, novels themselves.

Again, we can find an illuminating analogue for Meredith's interest in these moments in Anscombe's work on the descriptions of intentional action. She discusses the origins of the split that isolates Willoughby and Clara as a difference between an egoistic I "latching on to" the thing it holds a place for, and the descriptions that stand in for one another and "swallow each other up" when they are attached to an intentional action. In her article, "The First Person," Anscombe contradicts the assumption that a singular demonstrative, such as *this*, must have a referent, arguing instead that all *this* has to have, if used correctly, "is something that it latches on to": "Thus I may ask 'What's that figure standing in front of the rock, a man or a post?' and there may be no such object at all; but there is an appearance, a stain perhaps, or other marking of the rock face, which my 'that' latches on to. The referent that 'this' latches on to may coincide. . . . [b]ut they do not have to coincide, and the referent is the object of which the predicate is predicated where 'this' or 'that' is a subject."[28] Of course, *I* is like *this*, and while its meaning has to do with a system of reference and is secure against a *failure* of that reference, it is neither stable nor definite. Thinking *I* guarantees the existence and presence of its referent to consciousness, but it is a placeholder, not an identity proposition. It means *here* is the thing, the person "of whose action *this* idea of action is an idea, of whose movements *these* ideas of movement are ideas, of whose posture *this* idea of posture is the idea. And also, of which *these* intended actions, if carried out, will be the actions."[29] The "latching on to" is Anscombe's version of Willoughby's "home from the hunt." *I* casts around for a subject—one that an epistemological observation *does not show*—to connect to an idea of the action that *I* has not yet motivated. The structure of the scene of "latching on to" is determined, in that *I* has to look for a subject in order to grasp the thought of an action it could perform, but *finding* the subject that *I* latches on to is not determined, because *I* has, for that moment, no subject.

In her monograph on *Intention*, Anscombe negotiates this relationship between the mental event and the motive from inside one intentional action with many descriptions A—D, all of which could be said to be true. Each of these descriptions "swallows" up any other: "A's being done with B as intention does not mean that D is only indirectly the intention of A, as, if I press on something which is pressing on something . . . which is pressing against a wall, I am only indirectly pressing against the wall."[30] Anscombe uses "latching on to" and "swallowing up" to different ends, the first as a demonstrative in search of a referent, and the second as a referent waiting to be referenced, but both are used to make sense of an intentional action from the perspective of the character one is when one is intending and is asked to describe an intention in essential terms. If "home from the hunt" is Willoughby's understanding of an intentional action as a traveling with and toward, a latching on to an *I* that cannot fail to be there, Clara understands the screen he builds as one description of many testamentary sacrifices she will make, swallowing up the egoist's referent to his larger, totalizing intention. By staging and restaging the moments when Willoughby latches on to Clara and Clara sees him swallowing her up, Meredith will make the structure of the novel itself, and not just the images or the characters who use them, dependent on the building of descriptions. He will end *The Egoist* showing us how the increasing abstraction of Clara and Willoughby's positions enables substitutions within them, how these substitutions come to constitute the meaning of the descriptions that Clara and Willoughby have built, and how such substitutions can lead us—dynamically, weightlessly—out of their entrenchment.

Meredith tries to talk about the origins of substitutions in two radically different ways. The first occurs just after Clara has appealed to Willoughby and been refused. She and Laetitia Dale take a walk through the hills, and Clara lets the long-pining Laetitia in on her attempt to quit the match. After a brief discussion of Willoughby's first jilt (the ironically named Constantia Durham, who left him for an army officer), Laetitia sighs, "So noble a gentleman!" "'And it is,' added Clara, as if to support what she had said, 'a withering rebuke to me; I know him less, at least have not had so long an experience of him'" (*E*, 129). Laetitia reads jealousy into Clara's self-flagellating agreement, remembers that Willoughby once explained Clara's coldness to her as a "little feminine ailment, a want of comprehension of a perfect friendship," and resolves not to praise him too highly in Clara's company (*E*, 127). Clara compensates for Laetitia's disengagement with an "overflow" of tears: "Oh! Laetitia, my friend, I should have kissed you, and not made this exhibition of myself . . . if that idea of jealousy had not been in your head. You had it from him" (*E*, 131). And then, without the slightest indication from Laetitia herself, Clara proposes on Willoughby's behalf: "At last! I could wish . . . that is, if it were your wish. Yes, I could wish that. . . . I risk offending you. Do not let your delicacy take arms against me. I wish him happy in the only way that he can be made happy. There is my jealousy" (*E*, 132).

The egoism of this exchange isn't wholly lost on Laetitia, who marvels, "Miss Middleton, you have a dreadful power" (*E*, 133), or on critics of the novel, who write of Clara's "ruthlessly sac-rific[ing] Laetitia on the altar of [her] own freedom."[31] She of-fers Willoughby up for the only "happy" situation imaginable, but only if Laetitia wishes it too; Clara is negotiating as though Laetitia had incomplete information, when she does not, and Laetitia is being asked to agree to take on Willoughby and his flaws, but only for reasons that she is supposed to disavow. Her "wish" is a favor for Clara disguised as a plea to her own negated desire, and the result is a strange blend of desperation and black-mail that Meredith swears is wholly "unconscious" in Clara, who is acting on an evacuated, noncalculative impulse (*E*, 133).

The second scene that describes a substitutional intentional action does some of this work by repeating Clara's offer with a more complete sense of its aphoristic isolation. It does this in two ways, the first by situating the narrative as third-person reportage from a hidden and uninvolved source—a proxy for our omniscient narrator but wholly concerned with the said and done, rather than the endless descriptions we've previously ex-amined—and the second by overly investing in the object of the intentional action, making it the concrete "end" (or version) of the proposal. After a series of tempests with Clara, including the barely concealed escape attempt in the middle of a thunderstorm that brings her back to Patterne Hall and subjects them both to lurid rumors, Willoughby proposes to Laetitia in secret, prepared to break with Clara in the morning. He arranges a midnight meeting, but unknown to them both, Willoughby's ward Cross-jay overhears the entire conversation from under a coverlet. The brief paragraph before the reportage situates Crossjay on an ottoman, waking from a dream as he hears his name spoken "until, as at a blow, his heart knocked, he tightened himself, thought of bolting, and lay dead-still to throb and hearken" (*E*, 329). The tags of his narrative are nondescript ("a voice had said"; "was the answer"), and the pauses between lines of dialogue are filled with paralinguistic characterizations ("The accents were sharp with alarm"; "in a voice between supplication and menace"). Crossjay's record is by far the least "crafted" bit of prose in the novel and yet takes pains to be thoroughly, *differently* accurate about descriptions. He is so accurate, in fact, that a sustained joke at his expense goes unnoticed in the opening lines, which begin with Laetitia's entrance:

"I came to speak of Crossjay."
"Will you sit here, on the ottoman?"
"No, I cannot wait. I hoped I had heard Crossjay return. I would rather not sit down. May I entreat you to pardon him when he comes home?" . . .
"He shall be indemnified if he has had excess of punishment."
"I think I will say good night, Sir Willoughby."
"When freely and unreservedly you have given me your hand."
    (*E*, 329)

The joke, the sign that marks this text as decidedly different from the precocious self-awareness that suffuses the rest of the novel, is that Crossjay is hiding on the ottoman that Willoughby invites Laetitia to sit on; "Will you sit *here*" places us neatly above it just before they begin. After some coercive reminiscing—in which Willoughby reminds Laetitia of her abiding crush, recites lines of poetry she wrote him years before, and regrets that he had not been more attentive to the woman who is "my home and my temple"—he repeats the proposal:

"We are all older, I trust wiser. I am, I will own; much wiser. Wise at last! I offer you my hand."
    She did not reply.
    "I offer you my hand and name, Laetitia!"

No response.

"You think me bound in honor to another?"

She was mute.

"I am free. Thank heaven! I am free to choose my mate—the woman I have always loved! Freely and unreservedly, as I ask you to give your hand, I offer mine. You are the mistress of Patterne Hall; my wife!"

She had not a word. (*E*, 330)

Our grasp of these descriptions is virtually instinctive, given their dispassionate pitch; we are not Crossjay, whose experience is elided once the dialogue begins, a dialogue in which he has the highest stake, but we are also not *not* Crossjay, since the omniscience we've become accustomed to in the rest of the novel gives us a method we clearly don't have here. Willoughby's investment in Laetitia's acceptance is transparent: like the ideal intentional form we have seen in Wittgenstein and Anscombe, where the reason in the agent is also in the act, Willoughby's coercion enacts its own ends, and Meredith's style corresponds by doing exactly what it says it is doing. But it is conspicuous that what all of this transparency amounts to is a naked glut of description from an evacuated source. Willoughby anatomizes Laetitia's desire in a way that neither she nor anyone else has previously revealed, forcing her into a deeper and more stubborn silence than she has maintained, and heaping on the single position of his wife two separate and opposed characters, neither of whom particularly want to be there. And yet, while this represents a complete stylistic affront to the same proposal offered by Clara—where the position created for Willoughby's wife became a gap rather than a heap of contenders—the answer is the same. Laetitia refuses the place, and for similar reasons.

Willoughby's proposal is straddled by two other efforts to clear the way for her: a chapter called "In the Heart of the Egoist," which is a reported inner dialogue that Willoughby has with himself, and "The Lovers," a scene between Clara and Laetitia after the former leaves the position that the latter has yet to take up. Formally speaking, they function as a description of one completed, intentional action, an idea to release Clara and her effective substitution. The position is abandoned *as* it is refilled; Willoughby "latches on to" the position Laetitia should take up after two attempts to substitute her for Clara have been refused. The energy inside of this position is literalized as a frisson between Laetitia and Clara that Willoughby provokes at every point, but it is crucial to note that all of these characters are trafficking in and working through descriptions. Whatever literal void Clara leaves in Willoughby's life is completely overwritten by his conceptualization of it; by the end of the novel, Meredith seems to have become broadly interested in the ways descriptions of intentional action could motivate a novel as a whole, with or without the dynamism of character or plot. The benefits are obvious—descriptions lend themselves to Meredith's aphoristic style, they are built on images that stack up without developing, and they allow him to maintain a commitment to novel form through a procession of evacuated objects—but the ends of his intention will be frustrated by this form. In order for something that is both intentional and an action to happen in the novel and to end it, Meredith will have to ascribe descriptions to an agent.

Willoughby sees Clara as a liability similar in kind to her simultaneous position as both the object and companion of his particular path "home from the hunt": "his pride was his misery. . . . But he was too proud to submit to misery" (*E*, 323). The problem becomes clearer as the narration moves from his diagnosis to his strategy. "Clara must be given up," he decides,

> but not to one whose touch of her would be darts in the blood of the yielder, snakes in his bed: she must be given up to an extinguisher; to be the second wife of an old-fashioned semi-recluse, disgraced in his first. And were it publicly known that she had been cast off, and had fallen on old Vernon for a refuge, and part in spite, part in shame, part in desperation, part in a fit of good sense under the circumstances, espoused him, her beauty would not influence the world in its judgment. The world would know what to think. (*E*, 323)

The double reading of the phrase "espoused him," which is both a tag of attribution to Willoughby that stylizes the lines as quoted monologue in a *past* tense and an action Clara takes in Willoughby's imagination, marrying Vernon in *future* disgrace, drives a cut through the text that, in its irreducibility as anything other than a pair of conflicting, isolated descriptions, comes as near as possible to giving us the grounds of intentional action as a *contentless* proposition. What's more, that simultaneity figures "him" as Vernon *and* Willoughby, and makes "espousing" a saying *and* a doing—latching on to and swallowing up all of those differences that the analytic theory of intentional action (and Meredith himself) tries so hard to distinguish. Meredith is presenting to us, and in the depths of a highly personal series of strategies, the primacy of exchangeable substitutions in the harmonics of formal coherence. What this irreducibility does for Meredith, in other words, is not to particularize and dissociate, but to combine and universalize.

But when Clara attempts a similar act, trying once again to give Laetitia to Willoughby, her fondness for the building of the fact of a proposition implicates her as an agent in a way that she must own. The question becomes, how to self-substitute when the self who clears the place to be filled, and thus has to be identified with it, is the self being replaced? How can Clara become conceptually identified with a system that is about erasing her from it? This is a question prompted by the kind of synthesis that substitution is supposed to enact and resolve; Clara says both *here is the thing I am saying*, and *the thing I am saying is me*, and this attribution involves exactly the kind of epistemological knowledge that analytic philosophy's theory of descriptions tries to dodge.

When Clara visits Laetitia after she has been released from her engagement, and persuades the reluctant substitute to take her place, she verifies the "purity" of her intentions with, "Can it be that you have any doubt of the strength of his attachment? I have none. I have never had a doubt that it was the strongest of his feelings" (*E*, 408). Laetitia takes Willoughby up as a capitulation to Clara's description of the strength of his love, but her action is not a verification of it, or indeed, a verification of her attachment to him. Her reply to Clara, "Do you remember a walk we had one day together to the cottage?" is a reference to Clara's first proposal, a reply that substitutes all of Clara's own reasons for rejecting Willoughby for Laetitia's own (*E*, 408). Clara's response is the catch in her effort at substitution, the thing that will put her in charge of her own description of intentional action as the builder of a proposition. It's the recognition of herself in the builder, and the thing that keeps all substitutions from being equal:

> Help me to forget it—that day, and those days, and all those days! I should be glad to think I passed a time beneath the earth, and have risen again. I was the Egoist. I am sure, if I had been buried, I should not have stood up seeing myself more vilely stained, soiled, disfigured—oh! Help me to forget my conduct, Laetitia. He and I were unsuited—and I remember I blamed myself then. You and he are not: and now I can perceive the pride that can be felt in him. The worst that can be said is, that he schemes too much. (*E*, 409)

The description of being unsuited or positioned incorrectly is a disfigurement through death, a self-separation that opposes Clara in such a way that she becomes an egoist, latching on to her fragments in place of a whole, looking for its referent. The isolation of Meredith's descriptions is the thing that boxes her in; for all her attempts at reference, the increasing substitutionality of her position swallows her into a false coherence.

So, why does Meredith engineer Laetitia and substitution over leaving Willoughby alone with the one the egoist loves most? Clara's self-deprecating joke, "if I had been buried, I should not have stood up seeing myself more vilely stained," hinges on the care she takes to literalize her analogy. If she had been buried, she couldn't have gotten more vilely stained than she was when she behaved so badly that afternoon, and the proof would be plain if she saw herself rotting. Clara has at last made an accommodation for herself, blurring the space between the object and her interpretation of it. The separation between selves that we've pulled from her response is meaningfully closed for a moment; Clara will have to stand up out of her coffin to make the comparison she needs to make, but it won't have any meaning for her unless the counterfactual is also true, that she's not been buried but acted badly instead. Clara is speaking nonsense—"Help me to forget it" and everything that follows—and just as Willoughby has tried to extricate himself from egoistic misprision by being as direct and anatomizing as possible, but winds up sacrificing meaning into a contentless proposition, Clara's freedom has come at the expense of her own descriptive capacity.

The place where Meredith finally realizes the virtues of the descriptions of intentional action as a prime motivator of plot, a technique that leads him into the process of substitution that will make all descriptions irreducible to one another because they are decidedly interchangeable, is the place where Clara stands up and watches herself die. She has become the one through whom actions are described and understood, the ground and the corpse inside of it. To *make* meaning in this novel is to fill in the edges of Wittgenstein's snapshot, reading its details and darkness to see how intentions are in their acts. But to *be* meaning in this novel, to intend and distribute it, is to be an egoist, too easily attracted to the fact of propositions and not their objects, and identified with the descriptions you build, descriptions that negate and destroy. It is to misunderstand the accommodation as a thing that slides the object into its interpretation, instead of seeing much less, a darkness that says *here is the thing I am saying*. What we find in Meredith when we are no longer looking is the incredible energy of that darkness.

2

Throwing Things in Thackeray

Be as splendid, and as brave, and as odd as possible.
« WILLIAM MAKEPEACE THACKERAY, *Barry Lyndon* »

The Memoirs of Barry Lyndon, Esq. is a novel with, by, and about a hero, so being "as odd as possible" is as much about indivisibility as it is about quirk.[1] The chance to *be* odd rarely surfaces—in Thackeray and in everyday life—because "oddity" is a predication that assigns its subject to a preexisting class of odd things, while "being odd" takes up oddity as a subject and treats it as a thing one could, say, predicate *into*. People are routinely described as odd, and we make sense of the description by accommodating each new circumstance and applying new criteria under it; when Barry Lyndon is instructed to *be* "as odd as possible," it is thus with the expectation that he knows enough about the structure of predication to exploit it.[2] He does, and through his success, the novel dramatizes some of the ways in which we use language to pick out, sort, and interpret singular objects. In *The Phenomenology of Perception*, Maurice Merleau-Ponty provides us with an analogue for Barry's starting position. He argues that in order to think of a world as "the reason for all settings and the theatre of all patterns of behavior"—to orient oneself toward it as a hero to a tale—a bivalent "distance" must be set between the human and the thing that elicits his action; each situation must not become the totality of his being, but impinge on him "respectfully," and require from him not that he take up a series of positions with each new occasion but that he understand the generality that outlines them as plot. By giving up spontaneity for "preestablished circuits" of behavior, for a synthesis of the *in*-self and the *for*-self, Barry Lyndon the hero can plan his reactions to the world "on the periphery" of his existence, and take up, for example, "being odd" as an orientation beside which, and through which, he acts.[3]

Barry is involved in a precarious campaign for the fortune and heart of the widowed Lady Lyndon, who receives him as a "horrible monster" (*BL*, 207). That he should be "odd" in response is a strategy devised by the self-titled Chevalier de Balibari, an Ideas Man who frequently saves Barry from himself. "You have no imagination to invent such a character as I would make for you," he says—and moves to contain Barry's courage, swagger, and audacity within elaborate "plans of conduct" (*BL*, 206). If Barry is otherwise unable to clear the field of competitors around Lady Lyndon, he is instructed to make relentless use of oddity and its unswerving intention: "[W]rite to her at first in the undoubting tone of a lover who has every claim upon her . . . vowing despair, destruction, revenge, if she prove unfaithful. Frighten her—astonish her by some daring feat, which will let her see your indomitable resolution; you are the man to do it" (*BL*, 206). For Barry, being odd is not going to be about navigating a way through a special class of odd people, but about a special kind of navigation. He will occupy an uncategorizable position in the novel, and he will maintain a bivalent distance, if he conceives "oddity" as a class of prepredicated subjects that lies on the periphery of his being and intentionally relates to that class as a thing he can use. Of course, claiming any kind of canny abstraction for Barry Lyndon is tricky, because he is also conventionally strange; his oddity is depicted as congenital and self-destructive; his existence is made possible and perilous by it, and when he is not an unwitting narrator who condemns himself out of his own mouth, his erratic temperament threatens his own safety. But all Barry has to do is track his position in a field of possible suitors. He will get what he wants by being and not being himself at the same time, and he will be the hero, indivisibly "odd," when he is the only one left.

There is a reason for us to elaborate "being odd," not merely as a strategy for living but as a strategy for talking about living: it offers us a third way between two distinct forms of representationalism that have historically influenced the way we read novels like *Barry Lyndon* that employ "unreliable" narration. We are conceiving of "being odd" as a weapon that separates Barry from a class of known quantities while giving him a way of tactically moving through that class, a movement that we think is both egocentrically organized and intentionally directed. This conception of "being odd" challenges the kind of mediational epistemology that would say that Barry's knowledge of the world is formed through the mental representations he already has with respect to it, making his knowledge as skewed as his representations.[4] Our conception of "being odd" also challenges the kind of reductive phenomenology that would separate Barry's reality into determinate and indeterminate features: things about which he has sense data versus things that he may know, believe, hypothesize, or expect to be the case, but which are missing from the sensuous aspects of his experience. This knowledge would also be only half-true, since he frequently perceives unreal events through a doggedly optimistic aspect.[5] Conceiving of "being odd" as a narrativized organization of Barry's navigation through the world is explicitly borne out in the central conceit of the novel as well as in its composition and reception histories. Almost all of *Barry Lyndon*'s interest for readers has come from the tension between the "actual" events that he narrates and the deceptively oblique way he narrates them, and it is Thackeray's artistic execution of that discrepancy that has received the most critical attention. He finds a way between two kinds of epistemological representations, and the result is that Barry himself disappears from view, as though in his insistent fictionality he fades into the mechanics of a story he ceases to tell.

The reasons why readers are so tempted to dissect a character like Barry—the irrepressible, present-tense narrator of the novel that bears his name, so concerned with reporting everything that happens to him that no other person or place makes an impression—are curiously irresolvable. One reviewer's theory has it that while we all consider ourselves the protagonists of our own lives, it is "much pleasanter to consider oneself a man of sense and honour than a low-minded villain; and to one who wishes to do so, and knows how to set about it, it is quite as easy."[6] This theory of the novel makes "how to set about it" the lesson of *Barry Lyndon*, a gauge of how greatly and how often one can lie before imposing on oneself or, in Merleau-Ponty's terms, of the extent to which events can respectfully impinge on the human as hero before they "fill his whole field of action."[7] There is little evidence to suggest that *Barry Lyndon*'s scandalous subject matter weakened its reception, but after its run in *Fraser's Magazine* from January to December 1844, Thackeray's plan to produce a "handsome saleable volume at the end of the year" was scrapped.[8] His cousin Richard Bedingfield recollected that Thackeray "meant it to be good; but he had to cut it short, because he was afraid of the public,"[9] and in what amounts to a critique of its reception, Anthony Trollope writes that there is nothing in the novel to "shock or disgust," and that he "should be doing an injustice to Thackeray" if he left readers with the impression that *Barry Lyndon* "taught lessons tending to evil practice."[10] A complement to this theory—about the reasons why we are tempted to focus on the novel's conceit at the expense of its hero—is Thackeray's, who argued that Barry is too roguish to take seriously, that his effect is more palatable than his story. "Don't read 'Barry Lyndon'" he said to his daughter Ann Ritchie, "you won't like it." "Indeed," she writes, " it is scarcely a book to *like*, but one to admire and to wonder at for its consummate power and mastery. . . . He tells his own story so as to enlist every sympathy against himself, and yet all flows so plausibly, so glibly, that one can hardly explain how the effect is produced."[11] Ritchie reveals something about the novel that is both paradoxical and banal: the drive to explain an effect that we barely notice is the critical purpose of *Barry*

Lyndon, as well as the drive to deceive that motivates its hero, and because it represents a "mastery" of the form of the novel, it engages in the practice of literary criticism.

We should therefore try to allow "being odd" to make at least three interrelated impressions: it is an egocentrically organized way of intentionally directing oneself through the world, a way of descriptively narrating experience that is neither epistemological nor phenomenological, and an originary moment of literary criticism, in which the split between narrator and narrated becomes so imperceptible that the narrative courts its own constructedness. But despite our ability to grasp the contours and significance of this correlation of pairs, the middle terms that Thackeray mobilizes between them in *Barry Lyndon* fail to refer to anything at all. Grammatically, each of these aspects of the behavior that is "being odd" have a stake in the referentiality of empty descriptions: the set of "odd" subjects that Barry uses to struggle through his courtship of Lady Lyndon, the narrative that Barry fashions to contain and reveal his experience, and the cognitive fascination with form that evolves out of our instinctive sense of narrative discontinuity. The possibility that an empty expression could refer has a long history in the philosophy of language and literary theory. But I think that Thackeray's interest in "being odd" in *Barry Lyndon*—like Merleau-Ponty's interest in the collapsing of *in*-itself and *for*-itself intentionality into the circuitry of practical space—adds a new breadth to this history that hasn't been sufficiently discussed in either field, since it is the affective three-dimensionality of "being odd" that makes it such a powerful conceit. One of the objectives of this chapter is to understand the combinatory force of "being odd" as the cognitive apprehension of things in the world as revealed by their reference in language. This "as revealed" is the key to my interpretation, for, as we have seen, it is not merely apprehension, narration, and cognition that locate Barry in space, but their messy and often mistaken aggregation. Prying our way into the science of language, movement, and spatial orientation, our emphasis falls on the potential of empty referential descriptions to communicate Barry's peculiar organization of experience. I think this potential supports the complex rigor of containment that enables "being odd" to work; after all, Barry's navigation through the world of the novel and the sets of predicated subjects that comprise it manages to be both intentional and misleading, both object-directed and stray.

The unreliable slipperiness of Barry himself is what in effect makes the novel go. *Barry Lyndon* will show us that knowledge about the objective location of an object in space and time is both necessary and sufficient for its successful demonstrative identification in an egocentrically organized space. And Barry himself will show us that the interpretation of perceptual input necessary for behavioral output is done both by the body (in its object-directedness), and by language (in its semantic structure). And yet, while these two egocentrically organized referential systems appear to be two different models of the same network of behavioral cues, it is rather more useful to think of them as one compound way of articulating the meaning of the proper name as a potentially empty referent, located in a space whose demonstrative objects interpenetrate. Thus, the co-referring relationship that is the semantic articulation of objects in space is held in tension by the subject, whose own referent exists in the interval between grasping them and knowing what they are.

Characters in Thackeray's novels throw a lot of things—objects, words, looks, themselves, and each other—and this seems right, since so many of his novels are about enterprises and their trajectories. But for a cynic like Thackeray, who is so interested in tracking our wastes of time, our mechanical performances, and our bland observances of inconsequential things, the acts of throwing and being thrown are ways of tracking how one is in the world. Rather than pointing to the thing one wants to be, or effortlessly grasping the ready-to-hand, Thackeray's characters scramble and reach, and scratch and fade. "The best ink for Vanity Fair use would be one that faded utterly in a couple of days, and left the paper clean and blank, so that you might write on it to somebody else."[12] The fatalism of fading away corresponds with the fact that his characters so often think of themselves as thrown around like tiny puppets, not in some grand human struggle between greed and grace, but in the tiny margin between, say, ambition and meanness, or between aesthetic pursuits and domestic happiness. They write on something, and it disappears, and tracking the interval in between tells the story of how they are in the world.

Put another way, Thackeray is interested in the demonstrative identification of present objects instead of a descriptive identification of forthcoming ones. If an object is mentioned, it tends to be acted upon. Becky Sharp throws Johnson's *Dictionary* from the carriage window. Mr. Snob tells us not to "fling [ourselves] under the wheels" of the aristocracy in a slavish adoration of their habits and manners.[13] Pendennis tosses verses in his bed, and then after his first literary success, throws open his window to look out into the night, and then flings himself back down onto the bed, in a "posture of hope and submission."[14] Catherine Hall—the murderess of Thackeray's Newgate novel—poisons her ruiner after he successfully throws a punch at her face; he will later throw the poisoned glass of punch at same, and miss her. Each of these examples illustrates Thackeray's interest in throwing as a narrative device that both moves the story along and eddies it; these moments set a precedent that Thackeray will return to and enact over and over again. Becky could have found the language to describe herself in that dictionary, but she throws it back into the yard; Mr. Snob will return to the aristocracy and become a paradigm of our conventional understanding of snobs; Pendennis is repeatedly victimized by his fickle gift for writing; and Catherine will learn, however belatedly, that it is easier to sever heads than to dodge punches. In each case, the local instance of throwing discloses a larger logic at work in the novel. How they throw helps to teach us a lesson.

Some of these moments are big and character-defining, and some are small and indelibly weird, but for all of their weightlessness, these episodes of throwing and flinging and tossing bear so much narrative weight that they tend to plod. In the opening chapter of *Barry Lyndon*, Barry is bringing his cousin Nora home from a ball—he is in the saddle, and she is on the pillion behind him—and they have a tedious argument lasting several pages over the fact that Nora danced a set with her suitor Captain Quin at the ball instead of dancing with Barry himself. Thackeray somewhat confusingly couches this argument as a debate between objects—as a debate between the "saddle" and the "pillion"—and the overall effect is that a lifeless conversation becomes even more (that is to say, literally) lifeless. And since Barry is himself the narrator conjuring these descriptions, we can watch him starting to think of himself and Nora as objects.

The pillion kindly "points out" that Captain Quin is something of a catch, that he is a valiant soldier and a man of fashion, while Barry is still only a twelve-year-old boy. In an effort to soften this blow, she says, "You'll catch cold without a handkerchief," "to which the saddle only replied by grinding his teeth, and giving a lash to Daisy [his horse]." "Oh! mercy," replies the pillion, putting her arm around the saddle's waist, "you make Daisy rear and throw me, you careless creature, you!" (*BL*, 25). Then they come to a bridge; all we are told is that it "was an old high bridge, over a stream sufficiently deep and rocky" (*BL*, 27), and if that word "sufficiently" seems to stick in the phrase, that's because in a moment Barry will throw himself, his cousin Nora, and his horse Daisy into the water.

Barry says of Captain Quin, "I'll fight him with sword or with pistol, captain as he is. A man indeed! I'll fight any man, every man!" Nora says, after a beat, what if "you, who are such a hero, was passing over the bridge, and the inimy on the other side? . . . I've heard say that Captain Qui—" and Barry interrupts her, extra-diegetically:

> She never finished the word, for, maddened by the continual recurrence of that odious monosyllable, I shouted to her to "hold tight by my waist," and, giving Daisy the spur, in a minute sprung with Nora over the parapet into the deeper water below. I don't know why now, whether it was I wanted to drown myself and Nora, or to

perform an act that even Captain Quin should crane at, or whether I fancied that the enemy actually was in front of us, I can't tell now; but over I went. The horse sunk over his head, the girl screamed as she sunk, and screamed as she rose, and I landed her, half fainting, on the shore, where we were soon found by my uncle's people, who returned on hearing the screams. (*BL*, 27–28)

If we compare this lengthy back and forth between Nora and Barry with the description of the "sufficiently deep" stream he hurls them both into, we can see the discrepancy between the descriptions of the objects flung and the space into which they are flung as marked by two isolating principles. First, there is a drive to encircle Barry, Nora, and Daisy into a single, throwable object; I'm tempted to read the description that Barry gives Daisy the spur, and then sprung with Nora as an encasing palindrome. And second, the moment seems structured by a general narrative modeling that is constitutive of the episodic novel—the stream is "sufficient" for the use that will emerge, but there is no language about the moment that they hit the water—the describeable leaves off at the indication that the three of them "went" over the parapet. The relationship between the object flung and the space it is flung into is even further attenuated by the fact that Barry, writing in retrospect, still is unable to say why he threw Nora and himself into the stream. He entertains ideas that he might have wanted to kill himself, that he wanted to impress Captain Quin, and that he might have hallucinated an enemy on the other side. Each of these possibilities is rooted in a problem of reference: to kill oneself is to destroy the referent—the object flung; to perform the act for Quin, who is not there and will have had to hear the story at a remove from someone else entirely is to create a referent for someone else to refer to; and to hallucinate is to make reference to an absent or empty thing. So, the space that would normally be taken up by a description of intentional action has neither intention nor action inside of it. The ends of throwing an object in this scene are not to arrive somewhere else, or for that matter to throw something *away*, but to draw our attention to the possibilities of referring to an object through the act of throwing it.

It would be easy enough to claim that tracking where one is by throwing away what one has is what the novel *Barry Lyndon* is about. Barry is born of a disgraced, bankrupt family; he gets sent off to Dublin to make a name for himself; he falls into and out of military service, loses his money gambling, blackmails a rich widow into marrying him, spends her entire fortune, and dies in a debtors' prison. It is clear that the novel is obsessed with loss, and registering what one has in the losing of it. We should, however, complicate that view, because the idea of "throwing something away" requires both that we have a grasp on the object we are going to throw away and that we are throwing it as a means to an end, to put it away. If we look at what is actually happening to the thrown thing in this scene, it is clear that something in the throwing short-circuits a completed action.

The rest of this chapter is an effort to figure out what happens in the act of throwing. We will survey some terms and concepts from the theory of reference, especially the different ways in which reference is a kind of pointing or grasping. But the payoff of our close readings will lie in the analytic language that we pull from Thackeray himself. Thackeray adds the term *throwing* to the way we talk about reference. It is a figure for referring not to objects but to reference itself.

Conceiving of throwing as a reference to reference is crucial for a novel like *Barry Lyndon*, known for its unreliable narration. Narration, whether reliable or unreliable, "fixes" things, it seems to predate all reference, and it is the perspective from which all information flows. However, when understood through the throw, unreliable narration becomes a part of the larger performance of reference: Barry's success is also his failure, in that he knows how references work, he knows how to change or short-circuit them, but he is undone by the practice of referring, because in throwing things he always manages to throw them away. Barry is usually in charge of objects themselves—here the horse, himself, and Nora—as he is the one who throws them. But each object is comprised of several relations that build a reference in their adjacency. The pillion and the saddle are quite literally riding together—each object is contingent on not being the other object—but when the saddle replies to the pillion by lashing the horse or throwing them into the stream, their interdependence is interrupted, just as Barry and Nora's dialogue alights on the external object Quin. Quin, the signifying proper name, becomes "that odious monosyllable," and the pillion and the saddle disintegrate into the thrown thing, "the horse," "the girl," and "I." In throwing away Nora's act of referring to Quin, stopping her on the utterance of his name, Barry winds up tracking an abstract set of demonstrative descriptions, on the model of "that *x*."

We have gone through this moment in *Barry Lyndon* to get at whatever it is that throwing allows Barry and the narrative to say about what is around him. The novel is written as a memoir, and memoirs tend to be pretty airtight cases of reference, particularly since they are so grounded in an attention to being in the world. Why, then, is there such a discrepancy between Barry's attention to conversational detail and its interruption and the description of place (which is completely absent here), and intention (which remains indeterminate)? Why does the mechanism of reference seem important in this passage? How does a proper name like Quin become "that odious monosyllable," and how do we understand what Barry means by that phrase, and how might we see that the descriptive shift is interesting? When philosophers talk about the way we refer to objects, they tend to model that reference on the acts of pointing to something or grasping it, but while there are plenty of objects in this scene, the lack of a background for them to come out of, and the lack of an intention in handling them, indicates that something else is going on, that something else is enabling an attention to the way reference happens. The fact that throwing is productive of a different kind of meaning—a meaning that doesn't rely on intention or the description of a completed action—indicates that there may be something in throwing that does the work of referring differently. Focusing on the throw contributes to discussions about narration, fictionality, and realism, while remaining trained on the difference between modes of referring: rather than taking all of these objects as ends (Nora and Barry and Daisy the horse), throwing refers to referring itself.

Thackeray gestures toward a theory of throwing in his essay "Autour de mon chapeau," the twenty-eighth of his *Roundabout Papers*. He asks whether, when you have felt some profound emotion, have you not flung your hat out the window—and hasn't that hat cost you a pretty bit of money? And haven't you regretted its loss, connected its loss with the moment in your mind, and then connected the new hat to the old hat, and the new hat to the flinging? He begins the essay on the "noble tragic face" of a man who has paid too much for his hat. The grief-pang sends him staring blankly at the hat, and through the hat, "into the grief beyond." "Of course I cannot particularize the sum," says Thackeray, "but he had given too much for that hat. He felt he might have got the thing for less money. It was not the amount, I am sure it was the principle involved. He had been done: and a manly shame was upon him."[15] This dark knowledge—and not the object itself—will haunt the man, writes Thackeray, because the object sits inside of an arc of knowledge about what happens around it. In moments of great emotion, he writes,

> have you not looked at some indifferent object so? . . . Objects mingle dumbly with your grief, and remain afterwards connected with it in your mind. . . . [A] book which you were reading at the time when you received her farewell letter (how well you remember the paragraph afterwards—the shape of the words, and their position on the page!) . . . or the words you were writing when your mother came in and said it was all over—she was MARRIED—to that insignificant little rival at whom you have laughed a hundred times in her company."[16]

The man's see-through hat and the marks on the page are meant to be analogous, two instances of the same kind of referential act, but while both objects refer to particular spaces and the losses they contain, the act of defamiliarizing the language one reads or writes is not the same as holding and staring through the very hat that references what happened to it.

Thackeray takes these examples together, but they seem to represent two different ways in which we understand and refer to things. The first, the transparent hat, shows us how hard it is to refer to an object simply by grasping it; grasping is effortful and complicated here because the hat's transparency quite literally takes the man out of his moment and into a sequence of memories and associations that are involuntary and evacuating. The second way, the marks on the page, are something else, something more like pointing to an object. The indissoluble presence of the shape of the words and their position on the page are particularizing aspects that inter-associate, so that the margins, the spacing, and the idea of a real language behind it all contribute to the reference being made. But the question Thackeray asks about throwing a hat out of a window performs both acts at once: it occasions the loss of something that you will refer to later, attaching that moment to an object you hold and particularizing its loss in a broader space, such that its position in that space—soaring out into the world, at an optimal distance from a world full of objects that are not it—is a position that gives it its greatest significance.

One way we might understand Thackeray's use of throwing as a kind of reference—particularly throwing as contributing to a kind of coping with objects—is to map it onto a phenomenological characterization of objects that are pointed out and seen "for themselves," objects that are predicated or "given a definite character" when we point to them. On this view, *pointing* is the primary signification of assertion: when we point to something, we are absorbed in "coping" with it, we see it interpretatively as a usable thing. If we intend to cope with, say, a table, it is *as a table*; we intend to use it such that it refers to related objects (chairs, forks, napkins, etc.). Nora, in this model, points to the stream, asking Barry what he, a hero, would do,—with it, to it, in it—if the enemy were on the other side. She relates to the stream as a gulf that enables readiness while inhibiting escape, just as Barry copes with the stream as a stream by throwing the horse into it. But this is not the whole story of throwing in this scene from *Barry Lyndon,* because it extracts too much information from the little prose we have; we don't, of course, know that Barry thinks of the stream as a place for a horse. And it doesn't begin to tell us how coping happens, or what part of the thing the coping impulse is actually latching onto.

We get a slightly clearer sense of throwing as a means of tracking a reference when we combine the idea of pointing to the usable thing with a more analytical idea of the naming and definite descriptions of objects. Bertrand Russell argues that "the name of a thing is merely a means of pointing to the thing, and does not occur in what you are asserting, so that if one thing has two names, you make exactly the same assertion whichever of the names you use, provided they are not truncated descriptions."[17] What he means by that is that the only function of a genuine referring expression like "the *F* is *G*" is to point to an object in such a way that if its predicate is true, then the expression is true, and it successfully points to the object. Both the analytic and the phenomenological ideas of reference start with the idea that, in Hilary Putnam's phrase, "'meanings' just ain't in the head." But they disagree about whether absent things can contribute to our ability to reference something: coping with a table involves coping with it as a thing that also refers to absent cups and chairs, but Russell says that the absent table with its absent cups and chairs mustn't have anything to do with your ability to point to the actual table in front of you.

Philosopher Gareth Evans found a way of reconciling these positions—a way that recalls Thackeray's hat-throw. He reimagines the absent thing as a kind of vehicle, so that if we allowed the phrase "Let's call the girl who broke Barry's heart 'Nora,'" then every meaning of Nora would be *both* a way of referencing lots of associations (even absent ones) and at the same time would locate a particular thing that is not anything else. In other words, Evans imagines that reference—in this case a "descriptive name"—moves back and forth, like a shuttle. This figures the kind of work that throwing does in the horse scene from *Barry Lyndon* in three respects. First, Barry writes that he could have been hallucinating an enemy on the other side of that bridge, which means that he could have had an imaginary enemy in mind, but any actual pointing he would be doing would be false—and we know that even if it is false, it is still significant, still has meaning in its being false. Second, the novel shuttles between the idea that Barry is putting an end to the "odious monosyllable" and putting an end to Captain Quin, and their interdependence feels significant. And third, while the assertion, "Let's call the girl who broke Barry's heart 'Nora,'" may help us track the novel's attempt to work with reference, it also demonstrates the extent to which this is a novel about fictionality, about creating a potentially infelicitous reference that still has meaning. There is a creative freedom in a decision like "Let's call this that," and Barry is prone to craving that kind of freedom.

So the problem of creating or sustaining a felicitous reference is important for the kinds of work that throwing does, both in this scene and for this novel in particular. The problem of fictionality underlies all philosophies of reference and all writing, because there is always the question of how descriptions of things can strike us at all if we have no existent references in common with nonexistent ones. There may be nothing in our experience that answers to the word *pillion*. But the novel *Barry Lyndon* is *about* fictionality; its central conceit is its unreliable narrator and the tensions between the "actual" events that he narrates and the deceptively oblique way he narrates them. Indeed, the referential slide from Quin to "that odious monosyllable" is only funny because the novel's focalizer and its point of view are standing in the same place. As the novel moves on from this early moment on the bridge, it becomes even clearer to us that throwing is not only a way of referring to reference in *language*, it is also the key to understanding how one experiences the act of reference as a being in the world. Barry's physical trajectory through the world is in this way as much about throwing as his language.

The novel seems to be exploring the idea that throwing is a

bidirectional process of exchange—we throw things in order to take meaning away from them. This becomes clear in the middle of the novel, where Barry begins to, in a way, lose control of his horse, when his attempts to make money and a lucrative marriage start to go very, very wrong. In a footnote to the text that Thackeray later deleted, he writes, "It will be observed, in one or two other parts of his Memoirs, that whenever he is at an awkward pass, or does what the world does not usually consider respectable, a duel, in which is he victorious, is sure to ensue," and indeed Barry is repeatedly punched, kicked, thrown, brained, and bloodied (*BL*, 112). He calls himself a "puppet in the hands of Fate" (*BL*, 57). By ill-luck, Barry is "thrown" into bad company: he is "prey" to highwaymen and con artists; as a soldier, he falls into the "black-hole" of a recruiting wagon; he loses money after he falls into gambling with the sergeants and is thrown by dice throws; and when he is caught for desertion, the door to his hiding place is "flung" open, and Barry, realizing that "the game was up," "flings" down his knife, is "flung upon by the sergeants," and "thrown" to the ground (*BL*, 84). Even when he does some of the throwing, he is thrown himself; "I was often in liquor," he writes, "and when in that condition, what gentleman is master of himself? Perhaps I *did*, in this state, use my lady rather roughly, fling a glass or two at her, and call her by a few names that were not complimentary. I may have threatened her life (which it was obviously my interest not to take), and have frightened her, in word, considerably" (*BL*, 268). However, "When I flung the carving-knife at her son I was drunk, as every body present can testify" (*BL*, 252). If Barry throws a knife or a glass, we are meant to understand that it is because he is in turn thrown off while in his cups.

It is clear from these moments of throwing and being thrown that the novel often relies on a visceral relationship to the act of throwing that takes us nearer to the act of grasping something than the pointing and naming references that characterized Barry's earlier work with the bridge. Now that we have a better sense of both the aesthetic project that underlies Barry's narration and the many ways in which the novel furthers that project by playing on his status in the text as a thrown and throwing thing, we are able to appreciate why Barry might want to position himself in a physical relation to objects instead of developing a way of coping with them.

We may intuitively think about grasping something as a kind of physical version of pointing to it, a way of making clear the ostensive link between something pointed to and our reference to it. (Wittgenstein famously makes this point by asking what we are pointing at when we point to a piece of paper and say the word *paper*. Is it the shape of the page, the color of the page, the weight, the way it curls? The fact that the same indeterminacy arises when we pick up the paper and say the word *paper* is a good indication that pointing and grasping might do the same kind of ostensive work and have the same kind of limitations.) But we run up against a very important difference between pointing and grasping, which is that, as Merleau-Ponty writes, "From the outset, the grasping movement is magically at its completion; it can begin only by anticipating its end, since to disallow taking hold is sufficient to inhibit the action."[18] What he means is that while grasping and pointing are both ways of referring to objects, the act of pointing to and identifying a doorknob and the act of unreflexively turning it in order to go through the door involve two completely different processes. When we are employing a situational, motor-intentional understanding of space, we are usually holding onto something with only a dim awareness of its individual significance; these moments of holding are not cognitively motivated but instead contain in themselves a kind of visceral knowledge about the object. Recent work in physiological psychology has shown that there is a profound separation in the brain between the functions that allow us to identify abstract shapes and sizes and the functions that allow us to physically interact with them; one way that subjects bridge the two is by reaching out and tracking their physical approach to objects, just like one of Thackeray's throws.

As we have seen, pointing to things in order to reference them is something Barry does badly. His narration is unreliable, he has a tendency to abstract specific proper names into demonstrative descriptions like "that *x*," and he is often thwarted in his attempt to point to a goal and meet it. So, if he cannot point, and if he finds himself physically flung in company, why can't he just take hold of something and grasp it? Grasping is an option—it is, as the philosophy of language (and our own intuition) suggests, the "other way" of referencing something. But he cannot, for reasons that are interestingly characterological. Unlike pointing to things in an effort to cope with them, physically grasping something is an action that can't be faked. Merleau-Ponty argues that a normal subject performs actions, real or imagined, against a backdrop that can become immanent in the movement itself, sustaining it and inspiring it. Play-acting requires the essentializing movement, the dexterity that comes from a fluid relationship to things in the world; the subject does not throw herself entirely into a play-acting situation (e.g., performing a military salute), but makes a minimal effort at an essential gesture that is the whole movement.

Thus, although it could be said that Barry takes hold of the saddle and the pillion and the horse, we couldn't quite say that he *grasps* them. He does not have the fluidity or essentialism that a referential grasping action should perform, and the thing was held in order to let it go. The felicitousness of the grasp seems a rather crucial part of the process of reference for Merleau-Ponty, but it is a part that Barry's character does not accommodate. Barry routinely takes up disguises and pseudonyms in order to escape those he has swindled or indebted himself to; throughout the novel he amasses thirty-eight different names, twenty-two of which are self-ascribed, including the name "Captain Thunder," which he takes up during a robbing and kidnapping tear. He is not what Merleau-Ponty would call a normal subject, since he throws himself completely and programmatically into any play-acting role. He plays, but forgets that he is playing.

This kind of full-throated performance is particularly evident when Barry tries to get a grip on his life after all the flinging about and to take hold of his potential wife, the widowed Lady Lyndon. He writes,

> If I can once get my hold of a place, I keep it. . . . when I fasten on a man, nothing can induce me to release my hold: and I am left to myself, which is all the better. As I told Lady Lyndon in those days, with perfect sincerity, "I will never cease from following thee! Scorn I can bear, and have borne at thy hands. Indifference I can surmount; 'tis a rock which my energy will climb over, a magnet which attracts the dauntless iron of my soul!" . . . That is my way of fascinating women. . . . My object was to frighten her: to show her that what I wanted, that I dared; that what I dared, that I won; "Never hope to escape me, madam . . . Fly from me, and I will follow you, though it were to the gates of Hades." (*BL*, 191).

The grasp as an interleaving of possession and entitlement operates differently than that understood by Merleau-Ponty's normal subject, who commits only the essential, if total, grasping movement. Barry seems to take things up by first assuming the position in which the thing should be grasped, searching around for an identity that he may inhabit completely, before taking hold of the things he wants. When performing a grasp, Barry's whole body is involved; there is no objective sense of its movements or position. Merleau-Ponty writes as follows of the "bad grasper": "If the performance is interrupted, all his dexterity disappears. Once more kinetic initiative becomes impossible, the patient must first of all 'find his arm,' 'find,' by the preparatory movements, the gesture called for, and the gesture itself loses the melodic character which it presents in ordinary life, and becomes manifestly a collection of partial movements strung laboriously together."[19] When Lady Lyndon decides to leave the country to get out of Barry's way, he intercepts her letters and arrives the day before to welcome her. He says it is beyond his power to leave her, that while his heart has a pulse he must follow her. "It is *my fate*, your fate," he writes. "Cease to battle against it, and be mine" (*BL*, 232).

So Barry is as bad at grasping things as he is at pointing to them—he is essentialist but not easy; he is brute and flat in his grasping, and what there is of a process or system that constitutes the grasp is repeated rather than completed. Barry immerses himself in the grasp, until both Lady Lyndon's terror and her indifference make the same impression, receding into a flattened, almost empty space, with Barry, as he puts it, "left to himself." Rather than emerging from an active, positively present space, Barry sees all in the goal, as a system of qualities linked by some intelligible law or fate, free from a specific place or time. After successfully blackmailing Lady Lyndon's favorite suitor, Barry writes, "while he went into the back-ground, I came forward, and took good care that no other rivals should present them-selves" (*BL*, 220). To want is to dare, and to dare is to win, he writes; and it is the physicality of that want that registers, not as a picking one thing out of another, but as an effortful, motor-intentional urging toward it—the dare, a reach; the win, a hold.

Once Barry takes up Lady Lyndon for his own, throwing things becomes the dominant referential model. On their honey-moon—in fact, on the drive home—he stops the carriage to fling his new money among the laborers that work the estate. He "shaves away" the moats, drawbridges, and outer walls around the place with openings out into terraces and parterres, and cuts down twelve thousand pounds worth of timber. He empties also the main hall, turning out its old armor, and replacing it with fake antiques, whose "broken noses, limbs, and ugliness" make refer-ence to an empty authenticity. But in the same breath, each of these alterations is qualified by its subsequent value. The timber would have fetched three times the money in an earlier day, the statuary bought at 30,000 pounds later goes for only 300 guin-eas, and the landscaping draws cripplingly expensive lawsuits from family and neighbors. In this way, Barry self-consciously reads his throwing away as a process of reference, not simply to his new money, bad taste, or purchased status and titles, but also to the subsequent significance these objects will have. He highlights at every point how the process of making meaning out of these objects is a process of tracking his attempts to refer to them—often to refer to them as absent. Even the imagery he uses to describe these recalls pointing and grasping: "Every thing I touched crumbled in my hand," he writes; "every speculation I had failed. . . . I am, indeed, one of those born to make but not to keep fortunes" (*BL*, 247). He throws things as quickly as he gets them, and reads in that throwing what it means to be able to throw at all.

We see the meaningfulness of the sense of the object that is thrown at the end of the novel, as Barry's life comes into focus around his son Bryan, whom he uses both as a means to amassing fortune and the ends of it, as his heir. Barry's marriage to Lady Lyndon quickly disintegrates, and she refuses to sign the papers that would authorize his control over her estate. He responds by having Bryan taken away from her until she begs him to return the child at any cost. Barry offers these returning gestures in order to borrow against Lady Lyndon's annuities—he even borrows against her life—and the effect of it all is that Barry is consistently making the future disappear in an effort to make his throwing away appear significant. Bryan is killed soon after when he is thrown from his horse, and this tragedy, which Barry effectively glosses over in the novel, occasions the first successful instance of a tracking of reference to an absent (and thrown) object. First we hear Barry characterize his memory of Bryan in terms of grasping, learning what he has or had in the holding. Barry writes, "So powerful is the hold his memory has of me that I have never been able to forget him; his little spirit haunts me of nights on my restless, solitary pillow" (*BL*, 280). The memory has a hold on Barry, who becomes, in turn, the pillow on which the memory haunts him. Then he refers to Bryan as a pointing-out, as an object in its direct presentation, pieces coming together to particularize their referent. Barry writes, "Many a time, in the wildest and maddest company, as the bottle is going round, and the song and laugh roaring about, I am thinking of him" (*BL*, 280). The bottle, the song, and the laugh signal the memory from a fog of mad company both in which and through which he thinks of Bryan. And finally, in the throwing gesture that tracks the solitary object into an indeterminate space, Barry writes, "I have got a lock of his soft brown hair hanging round my breast now; it will accompany me to the dishonoured pauper's grave where soon, no doubt, Barry Lyndon's worn out old bones will be laid" (*BL*, 280).

There is a chiastic structure in the grasping and pointing references that is made explicit in that last line. Barry's memories have a hold on him, and the bottle that is particularized out of is also absorbed into the company that passes it on. But the last line, about the piece of Bryan's hair that will follow Barry's bones, not only dramatizes the outside/inside structure of reference— hair and bone, getting to the thing that has meaning inside of it—but also couches its trajectory into space and time as the essence of its meaning. This trajectory is a fiction, a projection of the end of Barry's life. And it occasions more fiction, since while it is located near the end of the novel, it is not *the* end of the novel. Barry will go on to tell the story of Bryan's death, his own separation from his wife, and his legal battles and imprisonment, and even then the novel won't end—another narrator will step in and explain that the manuscript is, alas, unfinished.

The throwing structure of reference in Thackeray, the tracking of objects into space, makes the novel go, but it also ultimately prevents the narrative from landing anywhere. *Barry Lyndon* works and is interesting precisely because we are forced to enjoy the *hows* of referring, not the *whats*; we cannot count on Barry's references, because we cannot believe that anything he says is the case. In the process, we become more invested in (or are simply thrown back upon) the structure of reference itself. But throwing is a doomed way to foreground the act of referring. As Barry learns rather too well, the lesson about throwing is that in those moments when the object's distance and difference from you are greatest, when the arc of the object is all you can see, you risk losing it entirely.

Thackeray takes the primary conceit of *Barry Lyndon*, of a rogue who "knows the price of everything, but the value of nothing,"[20] from the regional penny magazines he read on a tour of

Ireland in 1841–42, particularly the "Adventures of Mr. James Freeny,"[21] the pulpy autobiography of a highwayman that Thackeray later reviewed for *The Irish Sketch Book* (1845). Written with such a "noble naïveté and simplicity" that its hero depicts his "fearful duty" with the "utter unconsciousness that he is narrating anything wonderful,"[22] Freeny's characterization is regulated by the same formal logic that structures *Barry Lyndon*, whose hero confesses "I do not object to own that I am disposed to brag of my birth and other acquirements, for I have always found that if a man does not give himself a good word, his friends will not do it for him" (*BL*, 66). With a breezy candor evocative of *Jonathan Wild*, that "partaker of the imperfection of humanity,"[23] Freeny relates being attacked by, and single-handedly fending off, scores of "armies" while surrounded by crowds in thrall; he robs ten men on the highway in a single day; wins and loses great sums of money; sells and steals horses; and suffers three days in the woods with a bullet in his leg. Surprisingly, Thackeray's review of the "Adventures" ties the "grave simplicity" of Freeny's narration not to his marvelous self-characterization or its characterizing incidents, but to the range of moral corollaries it raises, each as dubious as the mind that finds it: "one may see the evil of drinking, another the harm of horse-racing, another the danger attendant on early marriage, a fourth the exceeding inconvenience as well as the hazard of the heroic highwayman's life," a "far better and more comfortable system of moralizing than that of the fable-books, where you are obliged to accept that story with the inevitable moral corollary that *will* stick close to it."[24] The particular lesson of the autobiography recedes further when we take Freeny's reflex courage into account, for his "serenity," "dexterity," and "dashing impetuosity" as the leader of a band of rogues—attributes Thackeray ascribes to his unconscious "presence of mind"—make a powerful case for caprice. Indeed, when Freeny learns his "men must fall," that "the world is too strong for us," he convinces himself to turn king's evidence and lay a trap for his associates, rationalizing that if all is indeed lost, "is it necessary that I should follow them too to the tree?"[25] Like

the "being odd" ethos that suffuses *Barry Lyndon*, Freeny's calcu-
lating "presence of mind" is built on a shallow, detached utility,
and this approach to the world allows him to make an exception
of himself and his "comfortable" read.

Freeny himself appears in *Barry Lyndon* as the first in a series
of grifters to sense Barry's simplicity and indicate it to us; in as
little as two paragraphs, the story Barry tells of their interaction
reads as a mixture of reportage and romance, a brief encounter
on a nameless road and bravery in the face of imminent peril.
After fleeing Castle Brady for Dublin under the suspicion that
he has fatally wounded his cousin Nora's now-husband, Quin
(widely regarded as the best she can do), Barry is described as
"falling in" with a "well-armed gentleman from Kilkenny, dressed
in green and gold cord, with a patch on his eye and riding a powerful mare. He asked me the questions of the day, and whither I
was bound, and whether my mother was not afraid on account
of the highwaymen to let one so young as myself travel?" Barry
brandishes his pistols, "that had already done execution and were
ready to do it again," but then, "a pock-marked man coming up,"
the gentleman "put spurs into his bay mare and left me" (*BL*, 50).
As Barry approaches Kilcullen to the cry of "Stop thief!" he
learns that his companion was none other than "the famous
Captain Freeny who, having bribed the jury to acquit him, two
days back, at Kilkenny assizes, had mounted his horse at the gaol
door, and the very next day had robbed two barristers who were
going the circuit" (*BL*, 37–38). The moment is revealing, because
Barry's being "obliged to give himself a good word" and Freeny's
implicating himself as one of a class of "highwaymen" enacts the
real difference between the single moral that sticks to the fable-
book and the many available to those who look for them. Barry's
sticky obligation to his character, Freeny's ambiguity, the pistols
with a suspect history, and the vague intervention of the pock-
marked man all restructure the bivalence of this scene through
its characters' complementary emptiness. Freeny is suspect because all we know is that he has an eye-patch and a mare; Barry
is suspect because his transparency leaves him no secrets—he is

empty on the page. In *The Irish Sketch Book*, Thackeray tells us that the residents of Kilkenny were told to "beware of a one-eyed man with a bay mare," and that indefinite *a* is important, not just because Freeny could be one man among several who fit the description, but because that class is another of the already-formed, unmysterious groups of "odd" people that Barry routinely works through. He recedes that content in order to revise his tale, and turns Freeny into an object even less expressive than the pistols he uses to fend him off.

Freeny and Barry both rely on a set of predicated subjects to navigate their way through the world, but they differ in the "being odd," or the "presence of mind," that constitutes that navigation. In his autobiography, Freeny's actions are constitutive of him; we never get the sense that his candor complicates his self-characterization, or that he ever misreads the structure of events that constitute it. During a confrontation with the owner of a house he is robbing, he writes, "I then demanded the key of his desk which stood in his room; he answered he had no key; upon which I said I had a very good key; at the same time giving it a stroke with the sledge" (*BL*, 159). Freeny's "utter unconsciousness" in this scene and others makes him blind to the deviance that Barry's legacy depends upon, and Thackeray's translation of his technique into *Barry Lyndon* means that the absence of Freeny's reportage, the absence of his "presence of mind," entails an absence of Freeny himself. On the other hand, Barry's reckless exaggerations of his birth and accomplishments reveal a narrative perversity that only "being odd" could make possible, and it is his position between intention and accident—between being, say, well-armed and well-defended—that defines his relation to and construction of the world as contingent.

This is what "being odd" as a kind of navigation has meant for Barry: a fluid distance from the world that remaps the particulars of its events into abstractions that he orients his way through, using his own egocentric relation to space.[26] Barry's attention is always lightly distributed: it is neither built of an association of objects nor a return to self-consciousness once those objects are conceptually controlled. Rather, it is an active reconstitution of new objects that picks them out of (and expresses their relation to) a once-indeterminate background. Barry's retrospective narration makes this orientation toward the world possible; Thackeray cannot show us the operation of this attention as Barry's *response* to Freeny's threat, but he can show us what would be missing without it, what it would look like for Barry to make himself available to Freeny's ambiguities.[27] Thus, what Thackeray takes from Freeny's autobiography is nothing less than the ability to reconstitute objects simply by alighting on them, to illustrate the ways in which noticing objects destroys those objects (and people-as-objects) by acting beside them. We do not, for example, know how physically proximate Barry and Freeny are when they meet on the highway; the description Barry gives of Freeny is generic, and his story is rewritten in retrospect and put into the mouths of the villagers at Kilcullen. And yet, Barry's ability to "track" his relationship to objects across these displacements, his ability to *be* Barry having a single interaction, tips us off that something else is happening in his experience that relocates the "utter unconsciousness" of Freeny's autobiography into the body's immanent relation to the world. Barry's alighting motor-intentionality enables him to "speak" through objects like pistols, patches, mares, and villagers; he locates himself in the scene with Freeny by referencing objects inside of it, but he distances himself from that scene by working through or beside those objects rather than using them in an intentionally directed way. They are crucial to any understanding of the "being odd" project behind the novel, which is why Thackeray's integration of the two autobiographies intensifies questions about the bivalent textuality of *Barry Lyndon* at the expense of Barry Lyndon himself; after all, the concept of "motor-intentionality" indicates action *and* intention, the roughly and lightly handled thing.

It is significant that the first word of "Autour de mon chapeau" is "NEVER," the *N* illuminated with a drawing that takes up two-thirds of the page. The drawing depicts a hunched, defeated-looking fellow leaning on a knobby walking stick and hauling a lumpy bag. He is wearing three hats of increasing size, stacked on top of one other; they are the darkest, thickest things in the drawing, and the heaviness communicated by their compounded weight—the heaviness that is produced by the iterative relation between them—seems to drive the man into the ground, his feet planted but disproportionately tiny, and his shadow seeped into the lightly indicated city on the horizon. The *N* itself is embroidered into the fabric of the highest hat; it is meant to latch onto "NEVER," but it recedes into the darkness of the drawing, such that one can only read the first sentence counterfactually as "EVER have I seen a more noble tragic face." The reader has to look for that "Never," but ultimately she has no reason to; at no point does the article itself make the distinction between *never* and *always* clear, and in fact the idea that the noble, tragic face in question is exceptional at all completely inverts the content of the article, which is about our universal tendency to physically handle those objects that stir our sense memories of absent people and events. Only by picking out and unpacking the image as an object on the page, a conspicuously black hole that the text has to wind around and accommodate, can we sense the exceptionality of the face, its referential singularity. And so, while Thackeray's article is theorizing what Merleau-Ponty will call our "motor-intentional" relationship to the world—consciousness, Merleau-Ponty writes, is "not a matter of 'I think that' but of 'I can,'"—it is this act of seeking out the proper name around which the article's theorization coalesces that will show us both how contingently and familiarly, how "Never" and "Ever," we reference things after we hold them.

Egocentrically organized systems of reference like Merleau-Ponty's are those that substitute for Cartesian coordinates "a knowledge of place which is reducible to a sort of co-existence with that place," such that "the subject conceives himself to be in the centre of a space (at its point of origin), with its co-ordinates given by the concepts 'up' and 'down,' 'left' and 'right', and 'in front' and 'behind.'"[28] Theorists of egocentrically organized systems of reference tend to agree that the content of our perceptual experience is nonconceptual, in that it irreducibly contains our dispositions to act bodily toward the objects we perceive: "The body's spatiality has no meaning of its own to distinguish it from objective spatiality."[29] In other words, there would be no space if I had no body, and it is in and through action that the spatiality of my body comes into being, that it *assumes* being; if a background were able to surround or extend outward from my figure in any meaningful way, I and it would have to partake of the same kind of being.[30] In *The Varieties of Reference*, philosopher Gareth Evans offers us a way of theorizing egocentrically organized systems of reference through the process of demonstrative thought, the ability to pick out and act on objects spatiotemporally. Evans borrows from Bertrand Russell the idea that a subject cannot make a judgment about something unless she knows which object her judgment is about, but he says that the knowledge of "which object" has to be "discriminating knowledge," that the subject has to have the capacity to distinguish that object from all other things *spatiotemporally*: she must know distinguishing facts about it that enable her to perceive it in the present and to recognize it if she is presented with it in the future.[31] Thus, identifying a place involves differentiating its spatial relations to the objects about which we have "discriminating knowledge," a simultaneous—that is, holistic—reference of its relations to each of the objects that constitute our frame of reference. Evans calls this kind of thinking about places a "cognitive map."[32] The cognitive map is meant to stress that this kind of thinking is at a certain level "objective," that annotations like "here" or "there" are not forced on us, because each place is represented in the same way as any other. This is not to say that being in the world in terms of the cognitive map is *omniscient* or third-person, because that would weight and affirm all places with an ideal verificationism; rather, "the thinking is truly objective—it is from no point of view."[33]

I think that Thackeray's novel *Barry Lyndon* plays with the distinction between Merleau-Ponty's and Evans's theorizations of egocentrically organized systems of reference, in that despite its resolutely first-person voice, the narrative itself lacks perspective, specifically a grounding sense of Barry's spatial position and his awareness of what it would mean to occupy that position. If we adopt Russell's principle, as Evans does, that thoughts depend for their content on the existence of the objects to which they refer, and that the semantically structured content of thoughts about those objects make demonstrative thoughts about them possible (and not simply the object to which they refer), then *Barry Lyndon* could be said to lack thoughts about things.

Evans refers to Russell's criterion for determining whether a term is singular—"Whenever the grammatical subject of a proposition can be supposed not to exist without rendering the proposition meaningless, it is plain that the grammatical subject is not a proper name, i.e., not a name directly representing some object"[34]—and takes from this the proposition that the semantic power of an expression affects its truth-value, and that the source of this power is determined by its referential connection to an extra-linguistic object. But in order to understand egocentric space as potentially organized on a cognitive map built of the simultaneous relations between objects about which we have discriminating knowledge, Evans has to reject the assumption behind Russell's Principle that there is no difference in the cognitive value of co-referring terms, terms that refer to the same object. If a thought is a thought *about* something, if it depends on the existence of the thing it refers to, then a cognitive map that has no point of view, that depends on an information link between objects and subjects, has to rely on the semantic value of that connection in order to track what he calls "discriminating knowledge" about those objects and subjects.

In one of the most important sections of *The Varieties of Reference*, which establishes "discriminating knowledge" as the centerpiece of Evans's theories of referential behavior, he defines discriminating knowledge as "the capacity to distinguish the object of [our] judgment from all other things."[35] In terms of the *fundamental ground of difference*, for spatiotemporal objects, this ground of difference is the object's spatial location at a time:

It seems to me that the idea of how objects of a given kind, *G*s, are distinguished from each other and from all other things must enter into our every conception of a state of affairs involving a *G*. For there is no thought about objects of a certain kind which does not presuppose the idea of *one* object of that kind, and the idea of one object of that kind must employ a general conception of the ways in which objects of that kind are differentiated from one another and from all other things. A conception of a state of affairs involving a *G* is such in virtue of its being a conception of a state of affairs involving an object conceived to be distinguished from other objects by some fundamental ground of difference appropriate to *G*s, and hence as distinguishable, or differentiable, by citing a fact of this kind.[36]

Evans's point is that the fundamental ground of difference for any given referent can be widely flung: statements such as "the man who made this table is a good carpenter," "the greatest prime number," or "this is H_2O" carve out a fundamental character of the object being perceived that—though it may, for example, be associated with the idea that H_2O is the stuff found in rivers and lakes—is perceived without necessarily being causally connected to previously stored information. If there is an alligator in my room, but I construct it as a singular term in my cognitive map, and navigate around it, all the while thinking of it as if it were a chair, then my perceptual experience of that alligator is qualitatively different than that of someone who perceives and refers to the alligator as an alligator. My thought may be *false*, but it is still a thought, in that it is subject to the idea that it holds a true or false value. In order for my statement about the chair to have any significance to the person who sees it as an alligator, we have to be thinking of the same object, but we do not have to think of that object in the same way; the way in which the semantic value of a singular term or referent is presented determines the sense it has, and so it can produce distinct thoughts.

Evans borrows this idea from Frege, and quotes Michael Dummett's observation that, "for Frege, we *say* what the referent of a word is, and thereby *show* what its sense is."[37] Evans, however, wants to make two inroads on Frege's thinking: he wants to complicate the idea that there are significant definite descriptions that do not have to have a referent—descriptions such as "the tooth fairy"—and he wants to do that by taking up Russell's Principle that if thoughts have to be about something, and propositions have to refer to singular terms, then we can create singular terms with demonstrative properties that bundle their semantic values in such a way that they produce a definite description. In this way, argues Evans, we can expand the conditions for understanding various kinds of singular terms.[38] Egocentric space models this kind of process of reference, since the referring expression that is the process of acting bodily on an object in a space is made possible by the network of discriminative thoughts that enable us to populate and navigate it.

The problem Evans is trying to solve with his insistence on the semantic thrust of an expression of reference as the sense it contains is that in several cases a definite description without a referent can nevertheless communicate a sense—this is, in fact, how we understand fictional references to Tristram Shandy, Elizabeth Bennett, and Lambert Strether—and if we were to combine the sense of a referent and the referent itself, as Russell does, then no statement about any nonexistent person would have any significance whatsoever. Russell writes,

> There is only one world, the "real" world: Shakespeare's imagination is part of it, and the thoughts that he had in writing Hamlet are real. . . . [b]ut it is of the very essence of fiction that only the thoughts, feelings, etc., in Shakespeare and his readers are real, and that there is not, in addition to them, an objective Hamlet. . . . If no one thought about Hamlet, there would be nothing left of him; if no one thought about Napoleon, he would have soon seen to it that some one did. The sense of reality is vital in logic, and whoever juggles with it by pretending that Hamlet has another kind of reality is doing a disservice to thought.[39]

Russell situates Hamlet in a class of "pseudo-objects" like unicorns, golden mountains, and round squares; unlike Meinong, who argued that there must be "unreal objects" if we can speak about them (and that in fact, because we can speak about them, there must be true propositions about which they are the subjects), Russell argues that we have come to the end of these objects when we begin to talk about them as singular terms, and that phrases like "a unicorn" do not describe something unreal, but describe nothing at all. Later philosophers like Ayer and Searle would solve this problem by completely disentangling sense and reference, arguing that it is irrelevant whether a singular term's referent has a sense, since different descriptive conditions, formed by the subject's entire personal history, impact the interpretation of a singular term. Neither one of these approaches suits Evans, who wants to argue that some representations are so related to their objects that, were the object not to exist, neither could its representation; although the contradictory expressions "David Copperfield was born in penury" and "David Copperfield does not exist" report at different worlds, they are *related* expressions for Evans, since they both give us singular terms that convey the content of a representation.

Barry Lyndon is a novel that repeatedly self-generates as a romance, an autobiography, a satire in the mode of *Jonathan Wild*, a piece of "magazinery," and a nod to Irish stereotypes. Indeed the structure of the book, reflected in the proper names of its various titles—first *Barry-Lynn*, then, on its publication in *Fraser's*, *The Luck of Barry Lyndon*, and then, on its revision, *The Memoirs of Barry Lyndon, Esq.*—is repeatedly substituting an abstraction for its subject, an abstraction that is semantically engineered to concretize a fictional referent. Thackeray writes in his notebooks about his difficulty drafting the novel, in entries that reiterate the self-generations of both its protagonist and narrative structure. On the twelfth of January, he writes, "Quite tired and weary with writing, which the evening's amusement did not cure. Wrote 'Barry Lyndon' for *Fraser* again—beginning, however, to flag . . ." A week later he writes, "In these days got through the fag-end of Chap. iv of 'Barry Lyndon' with a great deal of dullness, unwillingness, and labour." A month later he is "reading

for 'Barry Lyndon,' and writing, with extreme difficulty, a sheet."
Two days later, and trying to recuperate time, he writes, "Wrote
all day 'Barry Lyndon,' . . . continual labor annoys and excites me
too much." There is nothing more in the notebooks about the
novel's composition for six months, when on the tenth of August
he writes, "read for 'B.L.' all morning at the club," and then three
days later, "At home all day drawing and dawdling, with 'B.L.'
lying like a nightmare on my mind." August 19 he "wrote all day
'Barry Lyndon," and the next day, "wrote a little 'Barry Lyndon.'"
Thackeray leaves for a journey to the East (which will later become the rather more successful *Notes on a Journey from Cornhill
to Grand Cairo* in 1846) with *Barry Lyndon* "hanging round my
neck." In a final burst of productivity on November 1, he writes,
"Wrote 'Barry,' but slowly and with great difficulty," and on November 2, "Wrote 'Barry' with no more success than yesterday,"
and then on November 3, "Finished 'Barry' after great throes late
at night."[40]

There is much to be made of these references to "Barry Lyndon"
as a proper name, as a project, as an albatross, and as a nightmare,
but it's especially worth looking at the strange spatiotemporal
pairings of "wrote all day" with "wrote a little," or wrote "with
extreme difficulty, a sheet," and of course, "lying on my mind like
a nightmare," and the unusual ordering of "Finished 'Barry' after
great throes late at night" which begins at the end of the object,
produced after an action at the end of a time-space. But if we
look to chapter 4, the only one he specifically references in the
notebooks, we can see Thackeray repeatedly staging the problem
of reference, specifically the semantic delivery of the meaning
of an absent referent, and situating it as a problem of cognitive
mapping in egocentric space. Chapter 4, "In Which the Hero
Makes a False Start in the Genteel World," promises both the
unpacking of a definite description, "the Genteel World, "and
what it would mean to try to navigate it and fail. The chapter
opens on a new location for our protagonist Redmond Barry,
who, at sixteen, has left his uncle's home after a duel for Nora's
hand. Redmond thinks he has killed Quin, and is urged by all to

leave home for Dublin, to drop the surname Barry, and to call himself Barry Redmond of the Waterford County Redmonds. Barry promptly falls in with a couple he meets on the road, the Captain and Mrs. Fitzsimons, the first of several con artists to whom he will lose all of the money he has. Barry is impressed by tales of Mrs. Fitzsimons's "purse, containing upwards of a hundred guineas; her jewels, snuff-boxes, watches, and a pair of diamond shoe-buckles of the captain's," and he repeatedly interrupts his own narrative to reveal how he is positioning himself in relation to her things. He tells her he is "a young gentleman of large fortune (this was not true; but what is the use of crying bad fish?)," he tells her he has heard of her father, "(and though I had not, of course, I was too well-bred to say so)," and when her servant arrives at dinner and describes that a highwayman had subsequently returned her watch, "saying it was only pinchbeck," Barry confesses that he "took all of her stories for truth," and had he been "a little older in the world's experience, I should have begun to see that Madam Fitzsimons was not the person of fashion she pretended to be" (*BL*, 39). In the novel as a whole these kinds of positionings are fairly typical, since we are repeatedly struggling with the veracity of events as Barry relates them, but the parentheticals fragment the narrative in a way that seems honest; there is something about a narrative in pieces that appeals, stressing that the truth lies somewhere in the relation between the fragments.

What Thackeray calls the "fag-end" of the chapter is probably what appears just after this section, as Barry moves from the more specific terms of his gullible fall into a kind of blurry iniquity: "I purposely hurry over the description of my life, in which the incidents were painful, of no great interest except to my unlucky self, and in which my companions were certainly not of a kind befitting my quality." The Fitzsimons' intentions are revealed around the problem of reference, specifically Barry's pseudonym; the first indication that they are, as he will later call them, "adventurers and persons of no credit," is Captain Fitzsimons's gracious admission that "he knew the Redmonds of Waterford intimately well." This assertion is said to have "alarmed" Barry, for he knew nothing of them. But, he says, "I posed him, by asking *which* of the Redmonds he knew, for I had never heard his name in our family. He said, he 'knew the Redmonds of Redmonds-town.' 'Oh,' says I, 'mine are the Redmonds of Castle Redmond;' and so I put him off the scent" (*BL*, 39). A couple of days later, after Barry has finally lost all of his possessions, pawned those of several other people, and indebted his mare to a horse dealer, he returns home to find his valise open and his keys in Fitzsimons's hands. Barry writes, Fitzsimons "spoke of the fatal discovery of my real name on my linen," and compared it to the disguise written on Barry's IOUs, and "gathered up the linen clothes, silver toilette articles, and the rest of my gear, saying that she should step out that moment for an officer and give me up to the just revenge of the law." Barry's reaction to this discovery is oddly split: "During the first part of his speech, the thought of the imprudence of which I had been guilty, and the predicament in which I was plunged, had so puzzled and confounded me, that I had not uttered a word in reply to the fellow's abuse, but had stood quite dumb before him." Then, once Barry realizes the looming threat of danger, he claims to have changed his name to escape retribution for killing a man in "deadly combat," and threatens, "if you offer to let or to hinder me in the slightest way, the same arm which destroyed him is ready to punish you. . . . So saying, I drew my sword like lightening, and giving a 'ha! ha!' and a stamp with my foot, lounged it within an inch of Fitzsimons' heart, who started back and turned deadly pale, while his wife, with a scream, flung herself between us" (*BL*, 44).

This is a section in the novel that somewhat unsteadily bears the weight of Thackeray's effort. Barry "hurries over" his descent into bad company, book-ends its insignificance with specific, quoted scenes that dramatize the problem of maintaining a fictional referent, but at no point does the problem of fictional reference attach to Barry himself—instead, it is his things, his signatures on promises about objects, and his linens that betray him, and when he is found out, it is his "gear" that is gathered up as evidence for the law, instead of the person it betrays. It is Fitzsimons's "gathering up" of those objects that refer to Barry's proper name that shocks him into action, and the space in which that action takes place is only brought into focus because of that reference. Barry's foot stamp and lurch, movements that ground him in the room, and his grip on his sword, an object that effectively measures distance, generate the egocentric space in which Barry maps his interactions with objects through the references they bear with respect to one another. Evans writes, "I suggest that we take Frege's ascription of a sense to a Proper name to mean that not only must one think of an object—the referent of the term—in order to understand a sentence containing it, but also anyone who is to understand the sentence must think of the referent *in the same particular way*," and it's clear that the significance of Barry's deception is only brought into that particularity with the struggle over his things.[41] This is the minimal position: the content of demonstrative thought can be consistent with the conditions on having a thought at all, and gives us a reliable place to begin an analysis of *Barry Lyndon* as a theory of reference.[42]

3

Gaskell's Lost Objects

In the spring and summer of 1980, before he died of lung cancer at the age of thirty-four, Gareth Evans worked to prepare
his book on the philosophy of reference for publication. Chapters that were more or less written were extensively rewritten,
and chapters 6 and 7, "Demonstrative Identification" and "Self-
Identification," were roughly compiled from graduate lectures
given that year. Editor John McDowell, Evans's friend and colleague, writes that much of Evans's thinking in chapters 6 and 7
was "altogether new," and that Evans was rushing to draft a
"radical revision" of those chapters when he died in early August.
Throughout, McDowell's interpretation of Evans's manuscript is
silent; chapters 6 and 7 in particular are compiled from notes that
McDowell "worked . . . up into prose," with passages and ideas
Evans was dissatisfied with revised to reflect his later views; the
organization of individual sections is the product of "guesswork,"
and snatches of argument that could not be integrated into the
bulk of the material are sutured into footnotes and appendices.
"In all this," writes McDowell, "it seemed best to effect changes
without remarking on them, rather than to burden the text with
a complex apparatus of brackets and editorial footnotes."[1]

   Evans never titled his book, but he revised the title of a course
on the philosophy of reference from "The Essence of Reference"

to "The Varieties of Reference," on the logic that the course should provide a detailed investigation of *how* a conception of singular terms works rather than what a reference to a singular term *is*. As we will see, it is significant that McDowell is, by necessity, everywhere visible and nowhere identifiable in *The Varieties of Reference* (1982), disclosing the essence of Evans's argument without tracking the interventions he makes. Indeed, much that is claimed for the practice of reference in Evans's book can be usefully framed by the conditions of its publication. Moreover, the effort to produce a theory of reference that is removed from both the subject referring and the object referred to can be meaningfully unpacked by—and have powerful implications for—the structuring preoccupations of an altogether different kind of writing, the realist novel. While we know that realist novels can be cleaved off from other proximate genres because of their ability to generate references to things, often absent things, that have an order about them, what we have seen so far is that these novels are actually *about* the many *hows* of referring, the varieties rather than the essence of their references. McDowell's phrasing is useful here: finding the lost object—in one case Evans himself, in another, a letter, a toy, or a cat—presents us with the burden of capturing the sense of its difference from all other things, while challenging us to say just enough about how we came to pick it out. In a review of *The Varieties of Reference*, Stephen Schiffer writes that it "is not the book that Gareth Evans would have published had he lived."[2] This is the kind of sentence that would give Evans much to think about, and I believe that it could produce new thinking about the impact that referential logic has on the form of the realist novel.

The effect of McDowell's ghostwriting is felt most strongly in chapters 6 and 7, which gave him the least amount of material to work from, and the resulting change in style has an unsettling effect. A casual reader of McDowell's own prose would recognize his long, heavy clauses, notice that the chapters are twice as bulky, or that the appendices are either excerpts from previously published work or direct responses to Evans's thinking. So much of the force and relevance of Evans's argument depends upon the ideas presented in those chapters that it seemed to MacDowell appropriate to try to capture their argument without "excessive reverence" for the contours of their fragments (Evans, *VR*, v). This is somewhat uncanny, since the thoughts about particular, external objects that have dominated the argument of the book until chapter 6 (thoughts that Evans calls "'this'-thoughts") turn to thoughts about self-identification in chapters 6 and 7 (thoughts that Evans calls "'I'-thoughts"), and when Evans makes this turn, what he is in effect saying is that an idea of oneself must be built of the same stuff as an idea of an external object. Evans writes that a subject "must have the idea of himself as one object among others; and he must think of the relations between himself and objects he can see and act upon as relations of exactly the same kind as those he can see between pairs of objects he observes" (Evans, *VR*, 163). If somehow we were reading these lines without thinking of Evans himself as an object in relation or without thinking of Evans thinking of himself as such an object, he makes his position explicit:

> "I"-thoughts are not, as is sometimes suggested, restricted to thoughts about states of affairs "from the point of view of the subject." Nor can the thoughts I have been discussing be hived off from genuine self-conscious thought, for example by suggesting that by "I will die," I mean that Gareth Evans will die. Not at all; there is just as much of a gap between the knowledge that Gareth Evans will die and the self-conscious realization that I will die as there is between any thought to the effect that $ø$ is F and the self-conscious thought that I am F. It is not wholly inaccurate to say that I grasp such an eventuality by thinking of myself in the way that I think of others; this is just another way of saying that the fundamental level of thought about persons is involved. But it is of course essential that I am aware that the person of whom I am thinking *is myself*; certainly I must have in mind what it is for [$∂$ is dead] to be true, for arbitrary $∂$, but I must also have in mind what it is for [$∂ = I$] to be true. (Evans, *VR*, 210)

Several of these phrases cut too close to the bone to be ignored: "eventuality" and "realization" are dramatic examples, and the transition of the "*ø*" to "I" visually encodes the self as an empty set. But the phrases "I am *F*" and "arbitrary *∂*" are equally brutal, simply in virtue of their being such acute and dispassionate registers of Evans's own "state of affairs." The movement of Evans's prose supports this affective engagement; the force of his italics at the end of "the person of whom I am thinking *is myself*" knocks us over, and the neatly tucked-in "from the point of view of the subject" is flattened out into the word "Nor." (Evans often uses this rather bratty construction to break a discredited view.)

He turns himself into a case study more than once in the text, in sections he both rewrote and compiled, so we should be confident reading these references as Evans's way of incorporating—in the most literal sense—a lost thing into his logic, an incorporation that is deliberately in line with the self-presenting structure of his theory of reference. Evans earlier unpacks the demonstrative identification statement "That player will die of cancer" (Evans, *VR*, 148), and when he illustrates the idea that we can grasp propositions about ourselves even if we are "incapable of deciding, or even offering grounds for" them, he offers up some visceral cases: "I can grasp the thought that I was breast fed, for example, or that I was unhappy on my first birthday, or that I tossed and turned last night, or that I shall be dragged unconscious through the streets of Chicago, or that I shall die" (Evans, *VR*, 209). The "will die" and the "shall die" in these cases offer some narrative closure for the reader who is holding a posthumously published book, but they also reflect the meanings of sentences whose referents are unstable. When we read the embedded, anonymous "player" as actually picked out of his game to die "of cancer," this reading embraces "of" as a sign of both derivation and distance. And to say that the I that is unhappy, or tossed, or dragged, or a baby, or a bad sleeper, or in Chicago, "shall die," is a choice that refuses to conceptually delimit "shall," since it rings of intentions, plans, and expectations, which does the work of making it a proposition that can take more than one object, which Evans obviously intends.

Thus, we can read Evans's discussion of "I"-thoughts as the most trenchant iteration of the argument at the center of *The Varieties of Reference*, as well as its inevitable vanishing point. We have learned that what Evans calls the gap "between the knowledge that Gareth Evans will die and the self-conscious re-alization that I will die" is transferable to thoughts about being unconscious, being asleep, and being dead, in that we can of-fer no "grounds" for our ability to think them. We have learned that contending with this gap requires a conceptual "grasp" of the conditions under which we could think about them and of what it would mean to be able to satisfy those conditions. And we have learned that we therefore grasp an eventuality of the kind "I will die" by forming knowledge "at a fundamental level" about what it would mean for another person, an arbitrary ∂, to die, which, in turn, enables us to plug ourselves and others into an infinitely combinable series of discrete propositions. Once we possess the *concept* of death, in other words, we can make all kinds projec-tions that involve it. Evans calls this condition on reference the "Generality Constraint": If a subject can entertain the thought a is F, then she must have the conceptual resources for entertain-ing the thought that a is G, in however many ways of being G she can come up with: "Thus someone who thinks that John is happy and that Harry is happy exercises on two occasions the conceptual ability which we call "possessing the concept of hap-piness." And similarly someone who thinks that John is happy and that John is sad exercises on two occasions a single ability, the ability to think of, or think about, John" (Evans, *VR*, 101). The Generality Constraint is a kind of emplotment, in that it is built of a set of abilities rather than elements. If you understand that a is F, you can generate lines of thought like a is G, and a is H, but also that b is F and c is F, and so on. "This a is F" is a commutable point on a graph. And holding a posthumously published book by a writer who refers to his own death explicitly performs that commutability.

In order to understand why Evans's self-implicating use of the Generality Constraint is interpenetrated with the work that realism does in the novel, we must understand the intervention he is making. Evans is trying to account for how we intuitively understand propositions about empty singular terms, a class that entails fictional referents. We accept as intelligible the statement, "That novel that Jami has been analyzing sure sounds fascinating," even though, so far, "that novel that Jami has been analyzing" doesn't exist. Frege and Russell came to two complementary conclusions about the way propositions like this work, both of which Evans finds untenable.

Frege created a puzzle for himself in claiming that, because the referent of "That novel that Jami has been analyzing sure sounds fascinating" is coextensive with that of "That fictitious prose narrative that Jami has been discussing sure sounds fascinating," then these statements have the same meaning. But clearly, these statements can be differently understood; their "mode of presentation" is different. Since Frege's project is to define the shape of a public language, he had to revise his theory to incorporate the condition that in order to understand an utterance containing a singular term like *novel*, a person must not only think of a particular object, but think of it in a particular *way*. This way of understanding *novel* must be embedded in *novel*, it must travel with *novel*, and it must be the condition under which *novel* is understood. Frege calls the way we understand a term its "sense," and he comes to the conclusion that if we are going to have a thought about an utterance containing the term *novel*, then we have to understand its sense, so it must be this sense that *novel* refers to. The problem with this, as Evans sees it, is that Frege isn't telling us *how* we acquire a sense of things in the first place, and so proper names like "Urizen" may contain and communicate a sense without referring to anything. Frege tries to account for this with a theory of fictionality: thoughts about fictional, or "mock" objects produce "mock" thoughts. Such terms have a sense, but not the same kind of sense. This move is hedgy, if not fundamentally contradictory. The Generality Constraint gives us an airtight *process* of referring, so that a name can be descriptively introduced to us—"Urizen, according to Wikipedia, is the embodiment of conventional reason and law"—and then made available to any and all other thoughts that include "Urizen."

Russell did not believe that sentences like this one about Urizen are fictional; he thought they were "nonsense," by which he meant that they said nothing at all. This stringent criteria for the meaningfulness of propositions is entailed by Russell's more fundamental belief that in order for someone to have a thought about something, he or she has to know which particular thing in the world he or she is talking about. Russell's Principle stipulates that there are two ways of maintaining contact with such an object: either one is directly, or has a memory of being, acquainted with it ("demonstrative identification"), or one can think of it as uniquely satisfying a description ("descriptive identification"). Obviously, the idea that empty singular terms generate "nonsense" or are "fictional" is complicated for Evans by exactly the self-referring cases above: one can grasp a proposition about oneself such as "I will die" without being able to have grounds for it.

This leads Evans to two interrelated conclusions. The first he pulls from Frege: descriptive identification *cannot* satisfy Russell's Principle, because even if a singular term like "Urizen" is empty, the term may still have a sense, and the description that attaches to it may be understood. The second he finds in Russell: because the intention to use a demonstrative singular term cannot exist in a vacuum, the term must also engage a "demonstrative thought" in the listener. This means that the well-grounded utterance of the statement that "*a* is *F*" requires an audience who hears "that *a* is *F*, is what the speaker is saying" (Evans, *VR*, 306). The listener's thoughts *are* Russellian in that they must depend on her perceiving the object, too, but in order for her to think of the object in the particular *way* that the speaker presents it (Frege's point), she needs to have a discriminating conception of that object (Russell's Principle). This selective combination of criteria galvanizes "I will die" as crucial to Evans's thinking, and may be extended to any understanding of ungrounded references. The only way that Evans can understand the proposition that he will die is to be able to track the movement from knowing that a is F to knowing that a is G; "I will die" can be reliably projected if he is acquainted with a series or combination of concepts, so even if they are not directly visible to him, he can have thoughts about them. It is important that we see Evans's argument in *The Varieties of Reference* coming from the larger theories of Frege and Russell, because then we can see what he leaves out: Evans rejects the idea that we can have a theory of singular terms that ignores *how* we have them. We can't scapegoat fictionality: we can't rely on the truth-values of descriptive identifications when the descriptions themselves may do some of the work of referring just fine, and we shouldn't ignore the idea that thoughts can make connections in the same ways that demonstrative identifications can. The sequence from a to b to c and F to G that underwrites the Generality Constraint illuminates the fundamental ground of difference between objects in the world and the conditions under which they can be understood. So Evans says, yes, if we want to refer to something, we have to know which thing it is that we are referring to, but the way we know that is by *knowing what it means for a proposition about that object to be true.* And the Generality Constraint is built to show us that.

Thus far, I have taken the position that Evans's argument is about tracking ungrounded references, and yet the title of this chapter promises something slightly more dramatic in the finding of lost objects. The case for that drama is made, I think, in the examples Evans gives of his own death, which are not only moving in their implications, but are folded into a book that contains references to those implications on every page. The last sentences of Evans's introduction suggest that the study of self-identification in which the references appear was an initial gesture toward a broader investigation of what things are, such that they could be lost. Evans writes that, "like a cautious builder," he tried to make the work comprehensive, but goes on as follows: "However, there is one important limit that I have observed: I have ignored questions of *ontology*. I have not enquired into what it means to say, or how one might establish, that speakers have an ontology which comprises this or that kind of object. I have supposed myself to be working within a scheme of interpretation for the language which fixes the interpretation of, and hence fixes the objects capable of satisfying, its predicates; the questions which I want to discuss arise after these decisions have been made" (Evans, *VR*, 3).

If we characterize the question that ultimately eludes him as, What constitutes the object that can generate all of these propositions in the first place? we can see that what Evans fails to do is look at the "gap," the negative space between *a* and *b* and *c*, as possessing the capacity to meaningfully delimit *a* and *b* and *c*. The rest of this chapter posits that a study of that gap shows us how self-presenting objects associated through the Generality Constraint actually *are*. But by way of managing expectations, I should acknowledge that all of the readings of the gap that I initially considered and discarded are the ones my readers might be expecting. These readings include the following: reading gaps as necessarily positive (if they can't be negative); reading gaps as constitutive of the things they separate; and reading gaps as narratives that tell us of how particular objects get semantically grouped. Like Evans, I found that none of these readings actually tells us much about how we refer. Gaps are gaps, and we should leave them as they are. But novels can be *about* the gaps, and the cases they present have the particularity and concreteness of a case study. As such, they offer readymade what Evans worked to theorize: a "constraint" on generalities.

Elizabeth Gaskell's *Cranford*, which was published sporadically in Charles Dickens's magazine *Household Words* from December 1851 to May 1853 and then released as a single volume in June 1853, is currently everywhere. Since 2005, *Cranford* has been the focus of about fifty articles, dissertations, and book chapters, and the five-hour BBC series *Elizabeth Gaskell's Cranford* that aired from November to December 2007 was so popular that it produced a two-hour sequel, called *The Cranford Christmas Special* that aired in December 2009. *Cranford*'s investment in the nature of projectable things seems to have made it intensely available to two specific occasions: Christmastime, and the rise of thing theory in literary criticism.

The first episode of the novel appeared in the Christmas issue of *Household Words*, and generally speaking, the novel has a holiday spirit. As a compassionate portrait of old-fashioned women in a rural town, whose struggle with "elegant economy" necessitates descriptions of the stuff of domestic decorum,[3] *Cranford* traffics in the disposable markers of the passing of time that one sees shot through something like "A Christmas Carol." In fact, the first episode ends with a character reading "A Christmas Carol" "for a good long spell" just because it was "left on a table" (22). The repetition of time-sensitive routines like reading, dressing, knitting, letter-writing, and the conspicuous consumption of lots of tiny food measures the novel out in relatively interchangeable chunks, although we may agree with Andrew Miller that the repetition of habits in *Cranford* generates the movement of its two larger, linear plots. These plots are also about objects: one is about the failure of a bank, and one is a detective story involving a lost brother. Miller argues that "the indeterminate narrative structure which emerges from the juxtaposition of these linear and recursive forms" produces characters who "oscillate between two models of identity, one conventional and the other idiosyncratic."[4] This entailment is common for readers of sentimental novels, but it is also ultimately a little incomplete: objects that are threatening to become more than objects by potentially destabilizing the narrative's teleology are often ascribed "identities," and the fluctuations are thereby incorporated and understood as innately human. For example, one of Dickens's Christmas stories is called "Somebody's Luggage." This luggage—which is picked out for us simply because it belongs to nobody in particular and is neither discernibly singular nor plural—projects such a surfeit of associations that one wonders if tracking the misadventures of "the luggage that is somebody's" could lead us to a razor's edge between the unfamiliar and the intelligible. (It doesn't.)

The last line of *Cranford*—"We all love Miss Matty, and I

somehow think we are all of us better when she is near us" (160) —shows us how an opening premise like "the luggage that is somebody's" can get nailed to an occasion in a way that complicates our efforts to account for its instability. *Cranford* walks just a step or two ahead of the object it is memorializing here; the infinite sequence of possibilities open to it is tossed into "somehow," and therefore the question of *how* we refer that Evans would say undergirds the entire sequence of gaps and thoughts produced by a demonstrative identification is dismissed by an umbrella term, "nearness." The associative tracking of an object that gets aligned with everyday habits in *Cranford* is stuck to the kind of late-breaking gratitude characteristic of holiday fiction, and the result is a fuzzy claim about essences that self-presents as transitory and contingent. Unpacking this claim is the project of thing theory in literary criticism, an approach that would say that sentimentality is a criterion for and a condition of Miss Matty's place in the text. This final description of her as a "near" thing, according to thing theory, cashes out the habitual actions that mark time in the novel in favor of a quasi-memorialization that engorges the space and time between things in order to fill it in.

Is the rise of thing theory really comparable, as an occasion, to the coming of Christmas? Consider a story Bill Brown tells at the beginning of *A Sense of Things* about being in a poetry workshop: "Then—honestly—I started to write a poem, a Christmas poem: a joke, composed as a child's letter to Santa Claus that asked for things with ideas in them. The poem closed with the image of a small boy wildly unwrapping a package, then unwrapping the thing within the package, tearing away layers of plastic, wild-eyed to get to the idea."[5] The "occasion" is consistent with the objective behind this joke—"no ideas but in things" is something you *do*, and, like a joke itself, it is something that is done *to* you, too. Brown turns to a passage from Mark Twain's *Autobiography* to illustrate that finding the historical ontologies of things is structurally like an interpersonal encounter that, like the child with a gift, involves a slip from possession to identification. In this case, the *Autobiography* gives us a "textual occasion wherein, rather than bequeathing his house to his daughter, Twain grieves her loss through its loss":

> A man's house burns down. The smoking wreckage represents only a ruined home that was dear through the years of use and pleasant associations. By and by, as the days and weeks go on, first he misses this, then that, then the other thing. And when he casts about for it he finds that it was in that house. Always it is an *essential*—there was but one of its kind. . . . It will be years before the tale of lost essentials is complete, and not till then can he truly know the magnitude of his disaster.[6]

It is the *essential* quality of the lost object apprehended in the occasion of its magnitude that is most salient for Brown, as Twain "continues to identify with his daughter as the lost object, unwilling to detach himself, and he becomes increasingly aware of what within the object he has lost."[7] Twain is memorializing, melancholic, and is, like Brown himself, trying to find things to think with. For Brown, this occasion reveals to us a power in objects that can't be entirely epistemological.

John Plotz will direct this point at the Victorian novel in *Portable Property*, arguing that the novel is full of "properly doubled" objects, which are sentimentalized because they possess both a fiscal and transcendent value, rendering them "resonant but potentially marketable."[8] He uses *Cranford* to explain: "[Here] we find a novel defined by a virtual armory of objects moving readily between and among rival schemes of value, objects whose status as both commodities and inalienable possessions marked them out not as spoiled hybrids, but as ideal sites of sentiment. Two questions shape *Cranford*: first, what sort of possessions are endowed with the most sentimental meaning? Second, what relationship do such objects have to the dangerous world of promiscuous circulation?"[9] The "sentimental energy" of objects in *Cranford* is predicated on a meaning that is both particular to someone and capable of circulating as reified value, but the energy itself is largely produced in the process of gifting things that carry auras "by association" with the people who left them. Plotz calls this a "public form of portable privacy,"[10] and *Cranford* doesn't let us forget the privation in that privacy, the absent thing, or person, or event that invested the thing with value. Christina Lupton responds to Plotz, as well as similar work on things in *Cranford* by Adela Pinch, Elaine Freedgood, Hilary Schor, and Talia Schaffer, by mobilizing a reading of *Cranford* as "a test case for thing theory . . . because of its willingness to be read like the papers and fabrics that defy a distinction between sign and message at the level of its plot." She argues that the novel is an emergent "technotext" in that it speaks to its own materiality as a thicket of paper that is cut up, touched, and taken seriously in its material form.[11] This materiality, though it is said to "get beyond the dichotomies of sign and essence; depth and surface; metaphor and metonym," ultimately depends on viewing the surface of paper as an essence itself.[12] Lupton is taking up the point that history, consciousness, and subjectivity happen in contact with surfaces and textures. Cranford's failed banknotes are examined and passed around, "the hard reminder of failures of semiotic signification."[13] It is again the encounter with things that pulls the novel up against its own materiality as a social text and pulls readers into its narrative as characters themselves.

Evans's problem with ontology is not that it is indeterminate—things may be like humans and humans may be like things—or that some things can acquire a certain kind of conceptual "status" that makes them representable or exchangeable. Rather, Evans believes that all thinking that relies on ontological claims has limitations, and that any attention to spatiotemporal particulars should begin with "a scheme of interpretation for the language which fixes the interpretation of, and hence fixes the objects capable of satisfying, its predicates" (Evans, *VR*, 3). His approach isn't a rejection of the idea that objects can be interpreted as conveying different kinds of meaning (Frege's position is that objects can be differently meaningful given the different propositional attitudes of the speakers who are encountering them), and it certainly isn't a rejection of the idea that one can think of oneself as an object among other objects (we've read "Gareth Evans will die" in this way). Rather, what Evans means is that when an object has a property like "sentimental," or "lost," it only has that property because it is distinguished from other objects via some ground of difference appropriate to that property. Because the space between subjects and objects is so fluid in thing theory—Brown says that we are "possessed by our possessions"[14]—the encounter that arrests our attention to and fixes our interpretation of the objects that are capable of satisfying predicates like "is lost" or "is sentimental" often skirts the question of how we are able to refer to those objects in the first place. This is a serious problem for historical ontologies, especially if the objects that are the most available for that analysis, or are the most enthralling to its practitioners, are of a sort that lingers long after an occasion without being directly perceivable.

Cranford has been asked to map too many encounters with things to deserve a fresh inventory of its cups and saucers, so we will limit ourselves to some balls. About halfway through the novel, in a chapter disarmingly called "The Panic," a couple of robberies rock Cranford, and the women spend their evenings walking one another home and making regular expeditions around their kitchens with pokers, brushes, and shovels. One particularly candid evening, they share their darkest fears and the precautions they take to combat them. Our narrator, Mary Smith—who, as J. Hillis Miller has noted, capriciously widens and narrows the focus of her authority from "we" to "she" to "I"[15]—is afraid of "eyes—eyes looking at me, and watching me, glittering out from some dull flat wooden surface; and that if I dared to go up to my looking-glass when I was panic-stricken, I should certainly turn it round, with its back towards me, for fear of seeing eyes behind me looking out of the darkness" (98). The novel is obviously demonstrating a sensitivity to the way that perception works here, perhaps a way that implicates the commitments of its narrative voice—but there is a striking ground of difference between eyes "glittering out from some dull flat wooden surface" and eyes "looking out of the darkness," one pair in front, one behind. It is suggested here in the shared preposition *out*—why not *at me?*—that the gesture internal to Mary's story, turning the mirror to look away from the one who is looking, will only produce another set of eyes that glitter out at her through the back of the mirror, dull and flat though it is. It is suggested that the gap from one ground of difference to another is found in the "out" of something that we spin our mirrors to traverse. The route from the dull and flat to the darkness, from *a* to *b*, takes us through "out," through a mirror that, because its use is to expel the concept that one is being looked out at, to expel the "I" that looks at "me," is good for nothing *but* outs.

One of the reasons why we have to reject the idea that we could come to see these gaps as positive rather than negative spaces, or as narratives that tell us how particular objects get semantically grouped, is that here we have a gap unlike that between "Gareth Evans will die" and "I will die," or between "I will die" and "I will live." What we have instead is an irrational fear (that is not a hallucination) that doesn't demonstratively identify anything except maybe "my looking-glass," which is undone as a well-grounded identification even as it is uttered by the syllogistic "if I dared . . . I should." And yet the novel asserts that this fear has a very real semantic structure, hinged on the preposition "out," that enables us to imagine associations and to project the specific contingency that eyes could surface on the back of the mirror. But, crucially, Mary does not make that leap; we cannot be secure in the prediction that she has the ability to understand "indefinitely many" statements about this mirror, given the qualities she has attached to it. And this is a very strange claim, since "seeing eyes behind me" is so proximate to "seeing eyes behind my mirror," when "me" and "my mirror" are connected by the mirror's "back" and my "behind." The speaker is standing in the gap between these two eventualities, and yet when she grasps the mirror, it is only really "grasped" for us as a logical bridge between these two grounds of difference.

It should be said that the question of fictionality is largely immaterial for Evans. He treats novels in *The Varieties of Reference*, but he doesn't treat them as exceptional cases of demonstrative identification, where someone engaging in a conversation about what happens in a novel needs to have an understanding of the identity-conditions of its objects. For Evans, an utterance about what happens in a novel is just another site where one's ability to understand a proposition is projectible, given a set of objects and ideas about them (including, of course, the idea that one is reading a novel). This should inoculate us against the concern that the conditions of our applying the Generality Constraint to fictional texts are founded on or constitute a misconstrual. But it does enable us, in the same way that holding Evans's posthumous work enables us, to consider objects as lost in a particular way—not, that is, as things that possess us with our own investment in them, but as objects we can have thoughts about that include "there is a gap *here*," which let us know what it means to think those thoughts.

The description of Miss Matty's fear is much more specific, and her precaution is not only strange, but strangely projected in the novel. It will be productive here to take in the sequence as a single example, because fundamental identifications can only be made if an object is identified on a cognitive map that represents, simultaneously, the spatial relations of all of the objects constituting the frame of reference within which that identification is made. And as we have seen, the causal structure of precautions goes a long way toward revealing that frame of reference. After our narrator's confession, Miss Matty nerves herself up for her own:

> [E]ver since she had been a girl, she had dreaded being caught by her last leg, just as she was getting into bed, by some one concealed under it. . . . [I]t was very unpleasant to think of looking under a bed, and seeing a man concealed, with a great fierce face staring out at you; so she had bethought herself of something—perhaps I had noticed that she had told Martha to buy her a penny ball, such as children play with—and now she rolled this ball under the bed every night; if it came out on the other side, well and good; if not, she always took care to have her hand on the bell-rope. (98)

When the robbery panic has subsided, Matty turns the ball into a gift for the child of a famous magician. Matty is found "covering her penny ball—the ball that she used to roll under her bed—with gay-coloured worsted in rainbow stripes," and when asked why she is giving it to the magician's child, she says, "Although her father is a conjuror, she looks as if she had never had a good game of play in her life" (105). While she knits the ball over, she tells this story:

> "My father once made us," she began, "keep a diary in two columns: on one side we were to put down in the morning what we thought would be the course and events of the coming day, and at night we were to put down on the other side what really had happened. It would be to some people a rather sad way of telling their lives" —(a tear dropped upon my hand at these words)—"I don't mean that mine has been sad, only so very different to what I expected. . . . [D]o you know, I dream sometimes that I have a little child—always the same—a little girl of about two years old; she never grows older, though I have dreamt about her for many years. I don't think I ever dream of any words or sound she makes; she is very noiseless and still, but she comes to me when she is very sorry or very glad, and I have wakened with the clasp of her dear little arms around my neck. Only last night—perhaps because I had gone to sleep thinking of this ball for Phoebe—my little darling came in my dream, and put up her mouth to be kissed, just as I have seen real babies do to real mothers before going to bed. But all this is nonsense, dear! (107–8)

The ball rolled under the bed to mark the space where a man would be is covered in stripes for the child of a conjuror by a woman who conjures her own child, the child itself the trace object of a projection about Matty's life that is measured backwards, by her father, in columns. One might have found a way to say that more directly, but not much more directly, because even if there were a linear chronology to be sketched, the correlations within it that make it about one object do so in virtue of the gaps that exist between them—and the ball is tracking and measuring that gap.

Matty's diary frames the entire sequence as an exercise in referring to that which did *not* happen to her—there is no man under the bed, or under the sheets, and there is no child, no mouth, and no arms—but these lost things, lost as surely as anything else we have read, gain something by never having had a voice of their own, once they were predicated in the diary. The child's ball that disappears under the bed is so like the child's mouth put up to be kissed, just as the concealed man who might have given Matty a real child is mapped onto her dead father, and this connection is literally represented as a juxtaposition by the diary columns, one of the form "I will *x*," and one of the form "I did *y*," and by the ball, whose layered striping draws attention to it as an object that stood in for a leg by measuring the space under a bed, and now reveals "play" to a child, just as the column revealed wishes. These objects associate with one another via a sequence of propositions that is literally encoded in the text by a shifting interrelation of points on vertical and horizontal axes. The ball under the bed is overlaid with stripes; the columns are spliced with a horizontal narration of events that are both quotidian and monumental, or monumental because they are quotidian; the memory of the father's disenchanting frame of reference is occasioned by the wholeness of a ball whose stripes make it even more legible as round and full; and the sequence of events written into the diary have semantic organization that speaks the whole of their content (such that objects like the child will never speak). These constructions are founded on broader conceptual entailments about parents and children, visuality and tactility, and, generally speaking, the linguistic habits of Cranfordians. But the novel is content to ferment inside a gap between, say, "what we thought would happen in the course of a day" and "a good game of play," and pulls our attention toward the ways in which the conceptual apparatus that underlies the search for lost objects can itself be mobilized to tell a story.

There is a passage of Evans's that is irresistible to me, a passage that beautifully, sadistically explains what is at stake in these kinds of associative flights, because it is similarly built on another's expectations and disappointments. Imagine, he suggests, that on one day, a subject (let's call her Matty) briefly observes a wooden ball suspended from a crane, rotating around a fixed point, and on another day, she sees a different wooden ball suspended in the same place, rotating around the same point. She doesn't distinguish between the two balls—who would?—and then suddenly she falls down a flight of stairs, experiences a localized amnesia, and can't remember the first of the two days. Many years later, she reminisces about "that wooden ball" that she saw so long ago, but when pressed for discriminating information that would pick out the ball she saw, she is crushed to admit that she didn't know there were two. On the one hand, Matty is acting as though she subscribes to Russell's Principle, in that she thinks she has been in contact with a particular object and can pick it out; if she were informed that there were two different balls, she would obviously stop reminiscing about "that ball" as if she knew which one she meant. She would stop trusting herself to make that discrimination. And yet, says Evans, "it would certainly be quite natural, in view of the facts, to say that she was *thinking of* the second ball, or that she had the second ball *in mind*, or, if she spoke, that she *meant* the second ball" (Evans, *VR*, 90). The whole point of Evans's Generality Constraint is that we can retain the truth of our intuitive claim about what Matty has *meant* by establishing the several different relations in which subjects stand to objects, and unifying them via an associative sequence of concepts. And this can happen, crucially, even when the subject does not properly understand what she means because the object she is referring to is lost to her.

This last application of the Generality Constraint is a companion to the limit cases that Evans provides about his own death, since the subject under examination is unaware that she is exploiting a linguistic device she doesn't understand, as opposed to grasping a proposition about herself that she is "incapable of deciding, or even offering grounds for." She may, of course, be in the latter position once she learns she has been incorrect, but obviously there is a gap between them. There is a moment when Matty links up her thinking about the child and the ball by saying, "—perhaps because I had gone to sleep thinking of this ball for Phoebe—" and these dashes visually position her thought inside of a gap between the "perhaps" of her columned diary and the half-sleep, the "gone to sleep," of an ungrounded proposition. (Evans, we remember, offers the example "I tossed and turned last night" as just such a proposition.) The narrator's statement, "—perhaps I had noticed that she had told Martha to buy her a penny ball, such as children play with—" marks an important difference here, because it lacks the entailment "because." We have seen that the narrator has been incapable of grasping propositions like "back" and "behind," that depend on her separation between them, and here we could read her "had noticed" as a kind of incomplete attempt to insert herself between Matty, who "had told," and Martha, who had been told. The narrator's lost account of Martha's "been" is the place where we should end the study of gaps in *Cranford*, because to grasp what it means to refer to the thing we are referring to is to account for the fundamental ground of difference between things. It is to track the sequence of associations that tells us where we are in virtue of where we have been.

4

Murdoch and the Monolith

The first three chapters of this book discussed the ways in which different novels depict the challenges of referring to their objects, and in the process offer theories of reference that are extensible with those in the philosophy of language. In this chapter, I turn what we have been so far examining on its head: I treat an author who develops a theory of reference that, quite simply, *is the novel*. Iris Murdoch's fascination with the narrative potential of objects is explored in both her fiction and her philosophy. She is primarily interested in recovering the ethical for reference—in her eyes, evaluation is not something that lands on description but constitutes it—and so she pursues gestural modes of describing of the sort that make whole narratives into reference. If this book has so far treated cases of reference in the nineteenth-century realist novel, an analysis of Murdoch's work shows us not just that the study of reference is transportable to and recognizable in the literature of other periods, but that the kind of reading for reference at the core of *Object Lessons* has a wide application.

In her essay "The Idea of Perfection", Murdoch makes a case for the thingness of intention, arguing that a person's intention in saying or doing something—which would distinguish, say, between her acting in anger and her acting in shame—involves "the presence not of a particular private object, but of some typical outward behaviour pattern."[1] For Murdoch, this pattern of behavior is the novelist's most powerful tool, since the description of what happens is available to both characters and narratives, not closed off within some unknowable inner life. Her fiction places the idea of the empty intentional object squarely in an ethical register, arguing that the author has a moral obligation not to locate the motivations of her characters anywhere but in the description of the objects on which they act. But Murdoch is a conflicted inheritor of this realist tradition. Her frequent struggles with Wittgenstein's philosophy of language result in her committing to a view of the world as existing in an uneasy tension between fact and value, and the philosophical position she takes up in relation to it is thus predetermined by her resistance to Wittgenstein. Murdoch's vexed relationship to what she sees as Wittgenstein's totalizing view of the subject leads her to theorize *paraphrase* as an ethical act: she arrives at a radical theory of ethics grounded in action and gesture, but does so in reaction to him. In her fascination with the way characters both construct and are terrorized by myths, she shows us how actors can make any old thing into an intentional object, and how the description that gives characters the object as it is seen constitutes not only the plot but also the form of the novel, its own patterns of behavior. Martha Nussbaum writes that Murdoch repeatedly stages the negotiation between egotism and insight through explicit references to literary forms, from Plato and Dante to Freud and Wittgenstein; for Murdoch, the object of reference is literary form itself. She shifts easily from the form and content of representations of intentional action to the calculative articulations of the actions themselves, in an effort to illustrate the narrative's claim on intentional action.[2] Following Anscombe's suggestion that under some descriptions an action is intentional, and under others it is not, Murdoch understands an expression of intention as given by the description of the act under which it is intended: she understands, in other words, intention as a product of narration.

Given an introduction by Elizabeth Anscombe, Iris Murdoch met Wittgenstein just once, on Thursday, October 23, 1947. Upon arriving at Cambridge, Murdoch had surrounded herself with his disciples—including Anscombe, star pupil Yorick Smythies, the mathematician Georg Kreisel, and Wasfi Hijab, secretary of Wittgenstein's Moral Science Club—and they shared a single topic: "Wittgenstein, Wittgenstein, and Wittgenstein." In 1978 Murdoch would reflect, "How far has the fact that I have known *very well* certain people (Eliz, Yorick, Kreisel, Hijab) who were *imprinted* by Wittgenstein affected my work as a writer?"[3] Wittgenstein appears in some form or other (often by name) in most of her novels, including *The Flight from the Enchanter, Bruno's Dream, A Fairly Honourable Defeat, An Accidental Man, A Word Child, The Black Prince, The Philosopher's Pupil,* and *The Green Knight.* Throughout, one is impressed by her ambivalence toward him, expressed in her persistent struggle with the starkness of his philosophy of language and its scant interest in the social and psychological effects of a relativizing ethics.

Ultimately it is the cult of Wittgenstein that attracts Murdoch most strongly; his position as an organizing influence enables her to narrativize her ambivalence about his philosophy through what she sees as the paraphrasing distortions of groupthink. Wittgenstein's characterization of all speech—and all art—as "artful" and thus some form of life, is countered by Murdoch's own corrective attempt at a Platonism that would make art—particularly art that describes a shuttling back-and-forth between lofty ideals and moral ambiguities—the way to get at the truth about ethics. Wittgenstein's disciples misunderstand his position on art because they have been overawed by what she sees as his disenchantment with it, and in her recollection of her one and only meeting with Wittgenstein, the problem of paraphrase subtends everything else. According to biographer Peter Conradi, Wittgenstein said to Murdoch, "What's the good of having one philosophical discussion? It's like having one piano lesson": "He said to her, 'It's as if I have an apple tree in my garden & everyone is carting away the apples & sending them all over the world. And you ask: may I have an apple from your tree.' She remarked, 'Yes, but I'm never sure when I'm given an apple whether it really is from your tree.' 'True. I should say though they are not good apples . . .'"[4]

This is the kind of exchange with Wittgenstein that can inspire reams of commentary, revelation, and despair, but Murdoch's wariness of paraphrase here is characteristic. She argues that surrounding herself with disciples who have been "imprinted" by Wittgenstein must have had its own diffuse influence on her work, but the drive to get one true thing for oneself—to have *one* philosophical discussion at the origin—will run through her fiction as a troubling search, not for truth, whose elusiveness only produces the narrative's search for it, but for the *source* of truth. Characters in her novels rattle off Wittgenstein's proclamations as often as they reject them, but in each case it is the *act* of acceptance and disavowal that distinguishes these characters. In *Bruno's Dream*, the character Nigel lapses into conversations about selflessness that are littered with quotations from the *Tractatus*, and the novel *Nuns and Soldiers* begins:

"Wittgenstein—"
    "Yes?" said the Count.
    [. . . .]
    "He was sort of amateur, really."
    "Yes," said the Count. He was puzzled by Guy's sudden desire to belittle a thinker whom he had formerly admired. Perhaps he needed to feel that Wittgenstein too would not survive.[5]

The disavowal that must remain unexplained is typical of the thematic register of Murdoch's ambivalence, but it is also threaded into the fabric of her descriptive characterizations of Wittgenstein as illegible. In "The Idea of Perfection," Wittgenstein rests "sphinx-like" in the background of British empiricism;[6] while in *Metaphysics as a Guide to Morals* he is "a Martian staring at human affairs";[7] and in Murdoch's first novel, *Under the Net*, he exists as "a monolith: an unshaped and undivided stone which men before history had set up for some human purpose which would remain forever obscure."[8] This is ironic, since so much of Wittgenstein's contribution to the philosophy of language lies in his method of finding paraphrastic equivalents of sentences in which freighted terms occur, often terms of ethics such as "obligation," in order to reveal the essence of their misunderstanding in the misleading forms of natural language.

Murdoch's view of novel-writing is similar in that the novel's form is erected in order to be suggestive and incomplete. She says at one point that the novel is inherently comic in that it "belongs to an open world, a world of absurdity and loose ends and ignorance," and that while some novelists try to artificially lend it the significance of an enclosed object, "the nature of the novel, is somehow that a sort of wind blows through it and there are holes in it and the meaning of it partly seeps away into life."[9] This image of the novel appears in *Under the Net*. Jake, a failed writer himself but a translator of successful French novels, begins his next assignment by saying, "Starting a novel is opening a door on a misty landscape; you can still see very little but you can smell the earth and feel the wind blowing" (Murdoch, *UN*, 246). Jake enjoys translating because "it's like opening one's mouth and hearing someone else's voice emerge" (Murdoch, *UN*, 20), but he will be unable to translate this book because he feels as though he and its writer have been "entered for the same competition" (Murdoch, *UN*, 246). Like many of the writers in Murdoch's novels, Jake's sudden loss of his ability to channel and paraphrase other voices, brought on by a feeling of impending competition, marks a shift in his development as a character; like Murdoch herself at the meeting with Wittgenstein, the temptation Jake feels to see through a misty landscape is checked by a sense of its impenetrable capriciousness. Writing enables meaning to seep into life through its holes, and the world of the novel can be threateningly real through its doors. Murdoch glosses over the practice of paraphrase, the opening mouth at the threshold, and this is interesting because the potential for distortion is so high.

In *Metaphysics as a Guide to Morals*, she says that "at the border-lines of thought and language we can often 'see' what we cannot say: and have to *wait* and attempt to formulate for ourselves and convey to others our *experience* of what is initially beyond and hidden."[10] Murdoch is close here, but in the process of attempting to pinpoint how paraphrase works, she negates her position on the ineffability of formulated experience; "waiting," as we've seen in the opening lines to *Nuns and Soldiers*, is anathema to Guy's relationship to Wittgenstein, since "he needed to feel that Wittgenstein too would not survive." Even when she steps back to describe the role of literature in the world itself, this inability to describe the process of paraphrase holds. Here she speaks from the writer's perspective: "A deep motive for making litera-ture or art of any sort is the desire to defeat the formlessness of the world and cheer oneself up by constructing forms out of what might otherwise seem a mass of senseless rubble," and yet "[h]ow far reshaping involves offenses against truth is a prob-lem that any artist must face."[11] And here again, from the reader's perspective: "I think that people create myths about themselves and are then dominated by those myths." "They feel trapped, and they elect other people to play roles in their lives, to be gods or destroyers or something, and I think that this mythology is often very deep and very influential and secretive, and a novelist is revealing secrets of this sort."[12]

This chapter is an attempt to make intelligible the act of para-phrasing that figures Murdoch's relationship to analytic philos-ophy, both in her theories of ethics and aesthetics, and in her fiction. I draw from a range of her philosophical texts, since, al-though they are remarkably consistent in style, that style is, in an illuminating way, misspeaking the content of the texts. And I draw from her first novel, *Under the Net*, written while she was at Cambridge and deliberately engaged with the "problem" of Wittgenstein's philosophy and its mistranslation, because it is it-self an exercise in inconsistent form. I hope to pair these texts to illuminate what I take to be the central, and never acknowledged, tenet of Murdoch's philosophy of ethics: whether the world's secrets are revealed by authors to be encounters with a mythologized other or rubble formed offensively against truth, these actions on the world are predicated on a suspension of subjectivity. Murdoch's attempts to recuperate ethics and value as both the project of philosophy and the project of the novel ultimately rely on references to the intentionalities of subjects who cannot exist in the usual way.

I have cast the central problem Murdoch has with Wittgenstein in terms of her conflict between the usefulness of his philosophy of language and his compromised theory of ethics. This is a problem not simply because Wittgenstein addresses both subjects without resolving their mutual implications, but because for Murdoch these subjects have subsequently become indistinguishable in paraphrase. His refusal of the infallibility of self-knowledge "created a Void" as she calls it, that allowed relativism to be co-opted by neo-Kantians, existentialists, and utilitarians. In *Metaphysics as a Guide to Morals* she writes,

> A misleading though attractive distinction is made by many thinkers between fact and (moral) value. Roughly, the purpose of the distinction (as it is used by Kant and Wittgenstein for instance) is to *segregate* value in order to keep it pure and untainted, not derived from or mixed with empirical facts. This move, however, in time and as interpreted, may in effect result in a diminished, even perfunctory, account of morality, leading (with the increasing prestige of science) to a marginalization of "the ethical." (Big world of facts, little peripheral area of value.) This originally well-intentioned segregation then ignores an obvious and important aspect of human existence: the way in which almost all our concepts and activities involve evaluation.[13]

One of the intriguing things about this articulation of Murdoch's problem with the analytic separation of fact and value is the way she spatializes the misunderstanding of an "originally well-intentioned segregation" as a world ringed by a thin perimeter of ethics. While the result is consistent with the spirit of Wittgenstein's initial distinction, the representation she identifies as a spreading-out effects a marginalization of value. But the image she describes, punctuated as a parenthesis that hugs the big and little, is a self-presenting enclosure, and in that respect it prioritizes evaluation as something that concepts and activities shine *through*. So, just as Murdoch makes the case for the integration of ethics and action, going so far as to indicate that all behavior is in fact founded on our capacity for moral thought, she also in effect argues that action can become a vehicle for value.[14]

This is not the first time the image appears in Murdoch's philosophy. In a 1956 piece, "Vision and Choice in Morality," Murdoch argues against the analytic position that a contrived conceptual apparatus enables people to apply their different moral stances in language that avoids recourse to moral concepts. She writes that under this system, "Moral arguments will be possible where people have similar criteria of application (share descriptive meanings of moral terms) and differ about what exactly the facts are. Moral arguments will be difficult or impossible where the differences are differences of criteria":

> This picture seems plausible if we take as the centre of "the moral" the situation of a man making a definite choice (such as whether to join a political party) and defending it by reasons containing reference to facts. It seems less plausible when we attend to the notion of "moral being" as self-reflection of complex attitudes to life that are continuously displayed and elaborated in overt and inward speech but are not separable temporally into situations. Here moral differences look less like differences of choice, given the same facts, and more like differences of vision. In other words, a moral concept seems less like a movable and extensible ring laid down to cover a certain area of fact, and more like a total difference of *Gestalt*. We differ not only because we select different objects out of the same world but because we see different worlds.[15]

Murdoch displaces the distinction between moral value and facts onto the situation—the more discrete the scene, the more susceptible to descriptive criteria—but the situation is marked out by a ring of language rather than value. The ring is portable and capricious, and rather than a marginalization, it is the tool that enables the paraphrase of the facts it circumscribes. Again Murdoch's transparent punctuation—her parenthesis ringed around people who "(share descriptive meanings of moral terms)" and make discrete decisions "(such as whether to join a political party)"—illustrates her argument that, in this case, the analytic position is intensively rather than extensively organized. Murdoch favors a "continuousness" of moral attitudes, a recognition of their complexity, the integration of their overt and inward speech, and ultimately their characterization as an impressionable vision, and the point of all of this discursiveness is to expose the laying down of the ring as itself an expression of moral attitude on the part of analytic philosophers, to argue that the method of representation is itself a conceptual apparatus.

Of course, Murdoch is standing at some distance from both of the iterations of this image, mapping their epistemologies and narrating their casualties, and so when she writes about the relationship between freedom and determinism in the form of the *novel*, it isn't surprising that she returns to a similar representation. Here are three examples, the first an extension of the fact/value split we have seen so far smoothed into a discussion of the aesthetic; the second a statement about writing and plot; and the third a critical position on reading and character. In "The Sublime and the Good" she asks, "What distinguishes a moral judgment . . . from a statement of fact, or a judgment of taste," in effect arguing that both statements of fact and judgments of taste reference a single object that is arbitrarily distinguishable from itself.[16] In an interview with Frank Kermode in 1963, she says that in contemporary fiction, "there is a tendency . . . to produce a closely-coiled, carefully constructed object wherein the story rather than the people is the important thing. . . . [O]ften it turns out in the end that something about the structure of the world itself, the myth as it were of the work, has drawn all these people into a sort of spiral, or into a kind of form which ultimately is the form of one's own mind."[17]

Even when the construction of a novel goes well, she says—when, as she intends, the story of a novel encloses its characters—the contaminating form of the mind imposes a myth on the work that vertically pulls the specific coils of a story into a spiraling abstraction. In "The Sublime and the Beautiful Revisited," a reply to T. S. Eliot's denigration of nineteenth-century fiction, Murdoch praises George Eliot for her "godlike capacity for so respecting and loving her characters as to make them exist as free and separate beings," and underscores two senses of the word "free"—"independent of the author" and "independent-minded."[18] She develops this claim in a later interview where she praises George Eliot's world for being large and impersonal, "*the* world, where great art belongs."[19] Eliot solves the challenge of myth-making by displacing her personality onto those of her characters, and yet we are thrust out of this world to acknowledge its ostension, the "where" of great art. This collection of images isn't univocal, but it reinforces our sense of Murdoch's worries over the misunderstanding of concepts once they are paraphrased, ringed round with abstractions, abstractions that are in each case integral to their form. Freedom enclosed by a benevolent impersonality is misunderstood as a dreary moralism; novels enclosed by myth-making are misunderstood as a disinterest in character; and morality enclosed by judgment is misunderstood as inflexible.

There is something implicitly comic in being misunderstood in this way, both in Murdoch's philosophy and her fiction, because taking the trouble to impose a rational form on the formlessness of the world—be it a marginalized perimeter of moral value or a ring of meaning-rules—invariably leads to a messy non-universalizability. An oft-cited case she gives in order to assert the primacy of such mental events involves a mother (M) who feels hostility toward her daughter-in-law (D) because she feels her son has married beneath him. M's behavior toward D is flawlessly pleasant, but inside—that is, entirely in M's mind—a resentment is growing: "M finds D quite a good-hearted girl, but while not exactly common yet certainly unpolished and lacking in dignity and refinement. D is inclined to be pert and familiar, insufficiently ceremonious, brusque, sometimes positively rude, always tiresomely juvenile."[20] In time, and oppressed by her imprisonment within this view, M decides to reconsider her perspective, to see that D is "not vulgar but refreshingly simple, not undignified but spontaneous, not noisy but gay, not tiresomely juvenile but delightfully youthful."[21] Murdoch's greatest and most dearly held assertion is that (*a*) M is engaged in an internal struggle; (*b*) that this struggle informs and thickens being; (*c*) that it is the kind of action that is peculiarly M's own, an action without observers; and (*d*) that it therefore shows us that the world is *compellingly* present to the will. If one attends properly to the things of the world in all their complexity and particularity—if one approaches the world with "the idea of a just and loving gaze directed upon an individual reality"—then we take in the world with a vision that is itself moralized.[22] But the ubiquity of value means that our paraphrased descriptions of objects, people, and events can be so highly subjective and particularized that we have in effect rewritten the fact/value distinction, rejecting *its* criteria or attitudes in favor of the translation of something or other (a person, an idea, a choice, an object) into practical life.

This kind of translation lies in conflict with the recessive concept of "attention" that Murdoch borrows from Simone Weil's *Gravity and Grace*, described as a loss of egoism in the face of the reality of objects. Murdoch writes that "we can only understand others if we can to some extent share their contexts,"[23] and paying this kind of attention to them constitutes a form of *goodness*, "a refined and honest perception of what is really the case, a patient and just discernment and exploration of what confronts one."[24] Of course, for Weil, that kind of moral discipline evacuates subjectivity—attention must be "so full that the 'I' disappears"—and this is a loss so profound that even the dormant qualities of Murdoch's philosophical stance—"patience," "exploration," "confrontation"—would have to be rejected.[25] The way she gets around it is telling. If the problem with the analytic approach to the ethical is that it has marginalized value, *and/or* that it has laid an arbitrary ring around events, people, and objects in an effort to perform its random criteria of application (as we've seen, she's tried to have this image both ways), then it is only natural that she would paraphrase an extreme self-annihilation as yet another example of an off-the-page ethics, a refusal of reasons. And so it comes to this: rather than increasing her freedom by conceptualizing as many different possibilities for herself as she can, Murdoch promises that once her full and complete attention has been given, "I will have no choices and this is the ultimate condition to be aimed at."[26]

Before I turn to a fuller discussion of the fact/value distinction as it is paraphrased in her aesthetic practice, I want to return to Murdoch's depiction of an ethical stance. She gives us two models intended to work together. The first is of a circular area of fact, the things and people and events of the world ringed by value, or what she terms "the ethical." The value has been weakened and marginalized by, as she puts it, "the increasing prestige of science" into a perfunctory, haunted perimeter. Since she has elsewhere figured value as "attention," a selfless, just, and patient gaze, a thoroughly recessive refusal to engage reasons, Murdoch's enclosure of the active in the passive reveals itself, inadvertently resulting in an extensively organized ethical model. Fact has pushed value to the perimeter and keeps pushing: any action on the world carries with it an impression of moral value.

The second model presents us with the same circular area of fact, laid over with a portable ring of criteria. "To have criteria for something's being so," says Stanley Cavell, "is to know whether, in an individual case, the criteria do or do not apply."[27] According to Wittgenstein, all our knowledge is governed by criteria, even the capacity for judgments of both fact and value depend on the question of whether or not criteria exist to handle them. Given the consensual immediacy of criteria, this second ethical model can be read as an intensively organized enclosure, in which fact is pressured from without by meaning-rules. Both models are intended to describe the fall of value and complex evaluation, and to demonstrate the irrepressibility of subjectivity, but what happens instead is that both of these models cast action as a subjectivity. The annihilated self lends a patina of value to the dynamism of fact—"choosing" and intention—and the criteria that select and impress themselves on fact presuppose an application to judgments of value. Rather than showing us the place where value lies—and in effect the composition of value—she empties it out and refills it with forms that do the same job without the burden of subjectivity. Murdoch has inadvertently created two ethical models that elide the subjectivity they have been created to mark, and she substitutes for that subjectivity a superficial permeable value, as well as an incipient anticipation of moral judgment. Two models of subjectivity—one made significant by its spatial position, the other by its temporality—are in effect hosted by inanimate concepts.

In "Against Dryness," the essay in which she finally exposes her philosophical project as a theory of the novel, Murdoch characterizes our current assumptions about the "human personality" as "the joining of a materialistic behaviorism with a dramatic view of the individual as a solitary will" that manifests itself as a "structural dependence of concepts upon the public language in which they are framed."[28] For its part, the materialistic behaviorism emerges in this way: "Roughly: my inner life, for me just as for others, is identifiable as existing only through the application to it of public concepts, concepts which can only be constructed on the basis of overt behavior."[29] And the existentialism of the modern man as a "solitary will" is such that "his inner life is resolved into his acts and choices, and his beliefs, which are also acts, since a belief can only be identified through its expression."[30] For Murdoch, this post-Wittgensteinian hybrid of analytic and phenomenological philosophies of the self results in a man without a "rich receding background"—without the values or realities that surround and transcend him—and our depiction of this man (here is the implication for Murdoch's aesthetics) is indicative of what has become of "the connection between art and the moral life."[31] It has "languished because we are losing our sense of form and structure in the moral world itself."[32] While the nineteenth-century novelist "was concerned with real various individuals struggling in society," the twentieth-century novelist aims for "dryness," the "smallness, clearness, self-containedness" that she associates with T. S. Eliot, Paul Valéry, and Wittgenstein himself. "The pure, clean, self-contained symbol," she writes, "is the analogue of the lonely self-contained individual."[33]

Murdoch's understanding of the "rich receding background" is the "against" of "Against Dryness." It is the thing the novel does especially well, and it is the thing she suggests we plumb in order to recuperate "our sense of form and structure in the moral world itself." But the phrase "against dryness" derives most of its provocation from its confounding abstraction. We can assume that its recession is somehow related to "attention," especially in its Murdochian characterization as "not choosing," given the availability of her stance to accommodate the distance required to develop a sense of the moral world's "form and structure." Being in the background is conducive to a broad view. But clearly she also means something more, something "deeper," and if the reference to George Eliot holds, something active. In order to understand what's at stake for Murdoch in this concept, and to connect these two senses of *background* into a workable whole, I want to turn briefly to John Searle, who since the 1970s has been unpacking a strikingly similar phrase—"deep Background"—to similar ends, and whose most familiar illustration of this unpacking is performed on a passage from Murdoch's 1965 novel, *The Red and the Green.*

Searle coins the term in order to distinguish the innately human capacities for "walking, eating, grasping, perceiving, recognizing, and the preintentional stance that takes account of the solidity of things, and the independent existence of objects and other people" from what he calls "local Background," the situational knowledge involved in opening a door or chugging a bottle of beer. Both of these background capacities are preintentional and nonrepresentational for Searle; knowing "how to do things" and knowing "how things are" (Searle de-emphasizes that distinction) comprise what he calls "certain kinds of knowhow" that make intentional states and representational capacities possible. Desiring and believing are built on the framework of the Background, as are subsidiary intentions like "hopes and fears, anxieties and anticipations, feelings of frustration and satisfaction."[34] By way of an example, Searle argues that the belief that "larger states have more electoral votes than smaller states" is importantly different from and predicated upon the Background capacity for knowing that "people vote when awake." The former is part of a network of intentional states, while the latter appeals to a set of preintentional capacities.

Searle's Background tries to fill in the gap between the logical insufficiency of literal meaning and the conditions of satisfaction, to explain how speakers paraphrase and effectively comprehend the network of metaphors, ambiguities, and the other nonliteral, indirect speech acts shot through our descriptions. As philosopher David Sosa puts it, Searle's Background "is supposed to enable intentionality to function; in particular, it fills the representational lacuna. Its existence is then a precondition of a properly functioning intentional system."[35] So "deep Background" is a way of hiving off humanity's innate, biological capacity for *x* from both "local Background" action sequences and the network of intentional states, while at the same time illuminating the connections between truth conditions and literal meaning and mapping the systematicity of pragmatic competence.

One of the key implications for this work lies in the production and comprehension of a *fictional* speech act, which Searle describes as a set of "words and other elements" that have ordinary meanings, "and yet the rules that attach to those words and other elements and determine their meanings are not complied with."[36] A familiar way of putting this problem—a way of containing the problem but not the solution, he says—is to use phrases like "suspension of disbelief" or "mimesis." What we should be asking is "exactly how or exactly why" we suspend our disbelief, and what lies between the literal meaning of the words on the page and the conditions for satisfaction. To answer this question, he turns to a passage from Murdoch's *The Red and the Green*: "Ten more glorious days without horses! So thought Second Lieutenant Andrew Chase-White recently commissioned

in the distinguished regiment of King Edwards Horse, as he pottered contentedly in a garden on the outskirts of Dublin on a
sunny Sunday afternoon in April nineteen-sixteen."[37] With the
exception of the word "pottered," he says, all of the words in the
passage are meant to be taken as literal, but unlike the assertions of a nonfictional speech act, the propositions of the passage
are not taken for truth. Murdoch is not "committed" to them *as
true*. Since we cannot feasibly argue that fiction is made up of
a different set of illocutionary speech acts than nonfiction (because then words would have different meanings in fiction and it
would be impossible to understand them without paraphrasing
them as "new words"), then we have to assume that Murdoch is
"pretending" to make an assertion, "to engage in a performance
which is *as if* one were doing or being the thing . . . without any
intention to deceive."[38] Pretending is therefore intentional; it is
an illocutionary *stance*, a set of extralinguistic conventions that
resembles a Wittgensteinian language game, and it is Murdoch's
intention to suspend her commitments to the truth of her utterances that invokes these conventions and thus constitutes the
writing of fiction. So the gap between the literal meaning and
the conditions for satisfaction in fictional discourse is bridged
by an illocutionary stance that intentionally refuses one kind of
paraphrase (from old meaning into new meaning) for another
kind of paraphrase (pretending) that is characterized by a lack of
commitment to particular truth-conditions.

    Searle argues (somewhat paradoxically) that the Murdoch
passage was "deliberately chosen at random," but the choice is
fortuitous, given Murdoch's interest in the "rich receding background," her anxieties about translation and reception, and of
course the shared specter of Wittgenstein, whose language game
is neatly countered in Searle by the role that truth-conditions
have in the determination of fictionality. Searle specifies that
when Murdoch "pretends," she is not perpetrating an act of deception, but rather "acting as if she were making an assertion," or
"going through the motions of making an assertion," or "imitat-
ing the making of an assertion."[39] "Miss Murdoch," he writes, "is

engaging in a nondeceptive pseudoperformance which constitutes pretending to recount to us a series of events."[40] The weight
that Searle gives the question of deception in the pretense of
the illocutionary stance shows an attempt to come to terms with
the Murdochian tension between the "solitary will" and "public
concepts," the connection between "art and the moral life," and,
most of all, a rejection of the dryness of the "pure, clean, self-
contained symbol." Interestingly, when Murdoch *does* attempt to
convey a self-contained symbol, in the paradigm-referring form
of the proper name "Lieutenant Andrew Chase-White," Searle
argues that she is just *pretending* to refer: "One of the conditions
on the successful performance of the speech act of reference is
that there must exist an object that the speaker is referring to.
Thus by pretending to refer she pretends that there is an object
to be referred to. To the extent that we share the pretense, we will
also pretend that there is a lieutenant named Andrew Chase-
White living in Dublin in 1916."[41] Searle is saying that the author
creates fictional characters by pretending to refer to them, and
yet the "nondeceptiveness" of the "pseudoperformance" that constitutes this referential act is the thing that enables us to "share
the pretense" to whatever extent we do. Naturally, the greater the
extent—the greater the move away from the question of whether
or not there "is" such a character living in Dublin—the more successful the fiction. Searle even goes so far as to say that not all of
the references in fiction are pretended: "Some will be real references as in the passage from Miss Murdoch where she refers to
Dublin,"[42] and those real references enrich and enable us "to treat
the fictional story as an extension of our existing knowledge."[43]

In "How to Do Things with Austin and Searle," Stanley Fish
writes that Searle gets himself into trouble with these distinctions and, in opening the door to various and sundry species of
reference, manages to say nothing at all about what constitutes
fictional discourse: "That is, the category 'work of fiction' finally
has no content; one can say of it what Searle says of literature:
there is no trait or set of traits which all works of fiction have in
common and which could constitute the necessary and sufficient

conditions for being a work of fiction."⁴⁴ That is to say, the illocutionary stance of fiction invokes extralinguistic conventions
whose conditions of satisfaction are determined by the author's
responsibility to facts. Fish writes that when Searle speaks of the
shared pretense that creates a fictional character, he will be finally
saying something right if he subsequently acknowledges that *all*
communication is a set of collective agreements that make all
discourse fictional and serious at the same time.⁴⁵

Both Searle's and Fish's arguments pivot on the logical status of
the rules that are not complied with in fictional discourse—how
they are invoked, how they attach to or detach from the words
and other elements that comprise fiction, and how contingent
they are on our "existing knowledge" of the world. If we were to
cast our knowledge of these rules as preintentional Background,
as Searle would, we have come close to describing Murdoch's
"just and loving gaze," which, if we were to take the connection
as far as it could go, would mean that "attention" is also nonrepresentational and comprised of "certain kinds of know-how." If
we were to specify the signal thus interpreted by "attention," we
would see that signal as an intentional "pretending," and thus "attention" would be capable of discriminating reference from the
pretense at reference, facts from "facts," and therefore facts and
"values"—in short, the "form and structure of the moral world
itself." If Fish (along with Wittgenstein) is right, and all communication involves a certain kind of pretense, then this discrimination is both *incessant* and *constitutive*; Murdoch's ability to create
her fact/value models is only possible because value is marginalized. Not only does the gaze require an evacuation of subjectivity,
but it is built to descry and ultimately produce that evacuation.

This is a facile deconstruction of Murdoch's epistemology; at
one point in *Metaphysics as a Guide to Morals*, she describes Wittgenstein's "picture of the world (all the facts) as a self-contained
sphere, a sort of steel ball, outside which ineffable value roams,"
and we get the impression that she thinks of value as something
more than a blank stare.⁴⁶ What seems to motivate her certainty
that value is necessary to any description of the world of facts (no

matter how inconsistently it is described) is a horror of the alternative. She describes the "eerie feeling" she gets when she thinks of the background as an "empty box," a present-tense solipsism that requires outward criteria to distinguish its own emotions, thoughts, and morality. The past is a different country, and its *a prioricity* makes no claim on present sensations. The loneliness of waiting for criteria to come—she asks, "Can I know something (pain for instance) only from my own case?"—results in this despairing reading of Saul Kripke's assessment in *Wittgenstein on Rules and Private Language*. In a long passage excerpted by Murdoch, Kripke interprets Wittgenstein to say that "for each rule I follow there must be a criterion—other than simply what I say—by which another will judge that I am following the rule correctly. Applied to sensations, this seems to mean that there must be some 'natural expression,' or at any rate some external circumstances other than any mere inclination to say that this is the same sensation again, in virtue of which someone else can judge whether the sensation is present, and hence whether I have mastered the sensation term correctly."[47]

Murdoch's response is that "any view that supposes that, in this sense, an inner process always has 'outward criteria,' seems to me probably to be *empirically* false (Kripke's italics). This seems to me a welcome admission."[48] Given everything we know about the slipperiness of value descriptions as they appear in Murdoch's philosophy, we must take her at her word here, in the sense that the "empty box" full of pain, or something like it, shouldn't have to wait for a ring of criteria to land on it; it should heal itself. The question of what that would mean is left obscure; presumably one would be satisfied in the knowledge that private language *works*, that it infuses fact and value, or at least drills the kind of holes or openings out of the box that the novel always aims to be. The "mere inclination to say that this is the same sensation again" invokes the continuity that only narrative can bring, and so we could read Murdoch to be saying that a novel is like the box, what she calls the "inner thing," in that besides watching the world and itself at once, the disinterestedness of its gaze comes from a linearly constructed empiricism.

Before we turn to the integration of these theories in Murdoch's novel *Under the Net*, I want to make one other point about her essay "Against Dryness." "Against Dryness" opposes those novels that depict "real various individuals struggling in society," and those that depict "dryness," the "smallness, clearness, self-containedness" that "is the analogue of the lonely self-contained individual."[49] The empty box that waits for the criteria that will supervene on it is usefully fleshed out by Murdoch in her gloss on the term "self-containedness." "Self-containedness" meaningfully denatures the concept as an isolation, because the charge Murdoch levels at Wittgenstein is that "he seems to select, as illuminating special cases, examples of perception experience which are in fact hugely and vaguely ubiquitous." Rather, "The *experience* of seeing the approaching train (Merleau-Ponty's example) can, when released from phenomenology, be (as truthfully as possible) described in innumerable ways and involve innumerable considerations. (Is the train late? Will it be crowded? Will it stop? Will she be on it? Is it the blue one? Etc. etc.) 'Experience' has *layers*."[50] Murdoch sees herself carving out of the "ubiquitous" examples of perceptual experience that Wittgenstein reduces to simple "grammatical mistakes" those experiences of seeing that are not only innumerably particular to consciousness, but innumerably articulable. Here the pejorative "self-containedness" is not seen as the attempt to capture the nuances of experience in criteria but as the diffuse pressure of ubiquity, the idea that all experience can be gathered if the container is big enough. And all containedness is self-containedness if the language is public enough.

Again we see Murdoch's anxiety about paraphrase and groupthink imprinting her analysis of Wittgenstein's not-so-special cases, and so it is satisfying to see that what follows the declarative "'experience' has *layers*" is an argument with Wittgenstein about *copying*:

What about the "experience" of being guided or influenced, for instance in copying a figure. While being guided I notice nothing special. Afterwards if I wonder what happened I feel there must have been something else. "I have the feeling that what is essential about it is 'an experience of being influenced,' of a *connection*, . . . but I should not be willing to call any experienced phenomenon the 'experience of being influenced.' . . . I should like to say that I experienced the 'because', and yet I do not want to call any phenomenon 'the experience of the because.'". . . . Wittgenstein cannot find (and really does not want) any "because." The "experience" of being guided is an illusion.[51]

As we might have predicted, Murdoch will phrase her reply to Wittgenstein like this: "Can we experience an influence? Yes, of course, when (for instance) we sit wondering whether we have been wrongly persuaded by another person."[52] There is a real sense of alarm in this section about the experience of being swallowed up, not simply at the assumption of the particulars of experience into an anonymous bucket of sets, but more specifically at the subsumption of a person's individual philosophy into another, more totalizing one.

In an interview with Michael Bellamy in *Contemporary Literature*, Murdoch argues that Wittgenstein's philosophy is a nonphilosophy: "He says he doesn't have a particular philosophical theory, but he does have a way of looking at all philosophical theories." Bellamy asks a follow-up question: "I sense you feel this way about the so-called 'Wittgensteinians' in your fiction— those anal-retentive, pedantic types who quote his words without understanding the spirit in which he wrote them." Murdoch skips the characterological sketch in order to go straight to the issue of paraphrase: "I suppose I am myself, in a way, a Wittgensteinian; but if I am a Wittgensteinian, I am one in a proper, as it were, negative sense. It isn't that one has got any body of theory, but one has got a style and a way of looking at philosophical problems. He's a great philosopher."[53] I feel that perhaps we are getting closer to a systemic comprehension of the tensions we have seen in Murdoch's philosophy: her inadvertent elision of subjectivity and its replacement by a patina and/or presupposition of value; its mechanism as a preintentional background that discerns and creates its own elision; the novel as a loosely contained representation of the world whose influence on and by the real is never fully explained; and finally the box that waits for criteria instead of trusting its own past impressions, while suffering from an excess of description, a "fullness" of language always in danger of being swallowed up into a totalizing emptiness. If Murdoch's "proper" Wittgensteinian is *negative*—not in the sense that it negates his position, but in the sense that her gaze itself constitutes her philosophical stance—then we can see her applying all of the facts she could possibly alight on to practical life, stamped with the morality of her gaze. The philosophy she constructs is no longer a model at all, but a personal statement about the way she authors the world via her "way of looking," or "style."

Here we should turn to a novel like *Under the Net*, which gets its title from Wittgenstein's characterization, in the *Tractatus*, of the mechanism that contains and gives form to the particulars of the world. Murdoch will use this image as the signifying system that drives her novel. This is the passage that interests her: "Let us imagine a white surface with irregular black spots on it. We then say that whatever kind of picture these make, I can always approximate as closely as I wish to the description of it by covering the surface with a sufficiently fine square mesh, and then saying of every square whether it is black or white. In this way I shall have imposed a unified form on the description of the surface. The form is optional, since I could have achieved the same result by using a net with a triangular or hexagonal mesh."[54]

Murdoch says that her novel "plays with a philosophical idea . . . the problem of how far conceptualizing and theorizing, which from one point of view are absolutely essential, in fact divide you from the thing that is the object of theoretical attention."[55] Murdoch positions herself against Wittgenstein here, in that the net that is enabling for him is preventative for her, but what both of them can presumably agree on is that, as Wittgenstein writes, "In a proposition there must be exactly as many distinguishable parts as in the situation that it represents."[56] Language can only picture reality in the *Tractatus* by exhibiting the same logical form as the thing it depicts; the possibility of describing anything with a particular kind of net tells us nothing about the thing itself, except that it "can be described *completely* by a particular net with a *particular* size of mesh."[57] The picture theory amounts to a promise about its observational technique rather than the existence or nature of the thing it apprehends. The net is constitutive of the object for Murdoch in that it both reveals and conceals the thing, and this is reinforced by the idea that the net is engaged by the very kind of evaluation that she sees grounding all our understanding of the facts of the world.

Obviously, the net as Wittgenstein understands it affords us an unlimited number of interpretations of whatever state of affairs obtains, but when Murdoch creates her novel around the struggle of being "under the net" of discourse or looking "under the net" through discourse, especially when the net is a characterization of "conceptualizing and theorizing," she has recast Wittgenstein's image as something *gestural*, a performance not unlike that Searle finds in *The Red and the Green*, a "pretending" to refer that brings a fictional thing into being. The character Hugo Belfounder is an innocent whose philosophically provocative questions send our protagonist Jake into a metaphysical crisis; he says at one point, "We must be ruled by the situation itself and this is unutterably particular. Indeed it is something to which we can never get close enough, however hard we may try as it were to crawl under the net" (Murdoch, *UN*, 80–81). Wittgenstein arguably performs such "pretending to refer" himself when he speaks of "covering" the surface, but the net's enabling quality feels less like an effort to bring a fictional thing into being than an attempt to explain how we would use it. It is the tension between fact and value that motivates the narratives that are responsible for Murdoch's descriptions of the moral world, so ultimately it is the *obstacle* imposed by the net that is especially productive of fictionality. We should notice that the logical status of a gesture—a gesture like "crawling under the net"—is the thing that characterizes the shift from the philosophy of the *Tractatus* to that of the *Philosophical Investigations*. It forces Wittgenstein to admit that the thing that gives a sign its meaning is no longer its structural isomorphism with the signified, but instead its availability to criteria, rules, and judgments. If the act of evaluation is described by Murdoch as a gestural interaction with the net that divides us from the thing we are trying to pay attention to, then she has in effect created a fictional allegory for Wittgenstein's transition away from the picture theory of the *Tractatus*: gesture wrestles with the net of propositions that remake the facts of the world in its name. For Murdoch, evaluation is always off-the-page when we handle the world, resigned to a selfless trance of "attention" and/or a judgment of value latent in criteria, but here, in her fiction, it wrestles with the analytic approach to the facts of the world. Through its fictional reference, value finally gets to show up as an integral part of Murdoch's description of the world; however, she explicitly brings it into being it as an action *opposed to* "conceptualizing and theorizing," and opposed to their evacuated subjectivity.

Under the Net is explicit in its dramatization of the triumph of the gestural over language and criteria, and it stages the struggle between them as a practice of paraphrase. The novel hinges on two interactions between Jake and Hugo, the first chatty, the second silent, but at the heart of the novel is the paraphrase of their first discussion into a work of fiction, a dialogue entitled *The Silencer* that Jake writes behind Hugo's back. *The Silencer* starts as Jake's secret attempt to record their discussions, but as it grows into an analysis, Jake begins to see the book as Hugo's rival, and finally weary of both translating and competing with him, Jake breaks off with Hugo and publishes it. Their reconciliation years later is nearly wordless. Hugo has read the book and loves it, but doesn't recognize himself or his ideas. "His very otherness was to be sought not in himself but in myself," writes Jake, "Yet herein he recognized nothing of what he had made. He was a man without claims and without reflections"

(Murdoch, *UN*, 238). Writing about Hugo's presence in the novel is difficult because his scenes are so divorced from the rest of the plot; Murdoch herself called it "a freak novel" because "it lacks the maturity and the ability to construct in a more complex way, which I learnt later on."[58] L. R. Leavis says that Hugo Belfounder "seems included for local colour and to give depth to the narrator Jake," and that "a more natural reading of *Under the Net* only takes *The Silencer* as an intricacy of plot."[59] But the very freakishness of the novel makes Jake's conversations with Hugo all the more conspicuous as a negotiation between fact and value, both at the level of the novel's structure—Hugo appears as a dominant character only on pages 53–67 and 219–36—but also at the level of Murdoch's moral philosophy, where the evaluative crawl under the net is isolated from every other encounter with the facts of the world. The thing to look out for, the thing I have spent this chapter putting pressure on, is Murdoch's rendering of the act of paraphrasing, which has appeared as an epistemological gap—an opening mouth—in every aspect of her description of the divide between fact and value. My hope is that when evaluation is reintegrated into her model of moral value, its presence as an ethical action without a subject can be understood as the vanishing point of paraphrase.

Jake and Hugo meet at a cold-cure experiment, where they are both guinea pigs living in a country house, alternately injected with viruses. After two days of total silence—Hugo abruptly stops humming to himself once he realizes Jake has entered the room, which is "the nearest he seemed to get to acknowledging my presence"—Jake finally introduces himself and they begin long conversations (Murdoch, *UN*, 56). While we shouldn't put too much pressure on this moment, Hugo's decision to stop humming is in a way a refusal of the gesture, an early signal of its innateness in him, and a clue as to the novel's own conclusions about the role of evaluation in our apprehension of the world. Wittgenstein often writes about gestures in relation to music, both to understand how one is able to follow a specific piece of music through gestures, and to characterize the kind of thing that music is. In *Culture and Value* he states, "For me this musical phrase is a gesture. It insinuates itself into my life. I adopt it as my own."[60]

The discussions between Hugo and Jake are paraphrased from those Murdoch had with Yorick Smythies about Wittgenstein at Cambridge. Critics of the novel compare Hugo with Wittgenstein, but Murdoch herself acknowledged the reference to his protégé; biographer Peter Conradi quotes Murdoch as saying, "What a poor image of Yorick Hugo Belfounder is!"[61] This displacement allows her a freedom of interpretation and a staging of the resistance to a strong, totalizing mentor that direct quotation would not allow. It is productive to list some of these dialogues in order to get a sense of them, and I focus here on the passages that deal directly with the issue of referring descriptions and paraphrase:

> "There's something fishy about describing people's feelings," said Hugo. "All these descriptions are so dramatic."
>
> "What's wrong with that?" I said.
>
> "Only," said Hugo, "that it means that things are falsified from the start. If I say afterwards that I felt such and such, say that I felt 'apprehensive'—well, this just isn't true."
>
> "What do you mean?" I asked.
>
> "I didn't feel this," said Hugo. "I didn't feel anything of that kind at the time at all. This is just something I say afterwards."
>
> "But suppose I try hard to be accurate," I said.
>
> "One can't be," said Hugo. "The only hope is to avoid saying it. As soon as I start to describe, I'm done for. Try describing anything, our conversation for instance, and see how absolutely instinctively you . . ."
>
> "Touch it up?" I suggested.
>
> "It's deeper than that, said Hugo. "The language just won't let you present it as it really was" (Murdoch, *UN*, 59).[62]

Jake suggests that if all descriptions are false, perhaps people oughtn't to talk. Hugo agrees, with a caveat: "Well," he said, "I suppose *actions* don't lie" (Murdoch, *UN*, 60). It seems to me that there's little to unpack here, to the extent that we have seen

Murdoch's anxiety over the philosophy of language and its alienating ethical commitments, but there is something to be said for the fact that Hugo aligns action with language. He does so not simply as a substitute for language (for it is that, open to interpretation as much as speech), but, more than that, Murdoch's placing such weight on the moral implications of "lying," of the honesty of actions, seems in sympathy with her need for us to engage the net that prevents us from seeing things as they really are. Actions *connect* people. One of Hugo's converts, Jake's crush, Anna, says to him, "Love is not a feeling. It can be tested. Love is action, it is silence. It's not the emotional straining and scheming for possession that you used to think it was" (Murdoch, *UN*, 40), and in their final reconciliation, Hugo says to Jake "God is a task. God is a detail. It all lies close to your hand" (Murdoch, *UN*, 229). He reaches out for a glass and Jake remarks, "The light from the door glinted on the tumbler and seemed to find an answering flash in Hugo's eyes, as I tried in the darkness to see what they were saying" (Murdoch, *UN*, 229). For both Hugo and Anna, the description of emotional states in language is too lossy; it ought to be paraphrased in gesture. The lie of language isn't just a matter of "touching up," but an enclosure, since "language just won't let you" record experience. The repetition of the thematic and stylistic structure of the litanies "Love is action, it is silence" and "God is a task. God is a detail" is interesting because of their fundamental non-equivalence. Not only are actions and tasks governed by completely different conceptual aspects (the execution and a rule that governs it), but silence and detail combine to form Murdoch's single definition of "attention." This form thus makes actions and tasks co-extensive by being constitutive of "attention," which is then understood to exist in an action that combines parts, the exercise of details. Because we have to put these observations together—Murdoch dramatizes Jake's effort to "see" what Hugo and the light on the glass are saying to him— we are reminded of the role of paraphrase in our apprehension of the world as containing both fact and value. This configuration echoes the model we have seen so far at work in Murdoch's philosophy: we have to drag the pieces of value together to form one practice of "attention," only to have it dependent on action and tasks. The thing that her fiction gives us that her philosophy does not is the opportunity to watch her dramatize the subsumption of evaluation through paraphrase into action and language.

Jake and Hugo reconnect at the end of the novel, this time in a hospital, where Hugo has been admitted for a head injury. Jake remarks that "[h]is bandaged head was silhouetted in the light from the little window; I could not see his expression," and later "I could see Hugo looking at me intently. The bulky bandage gave him an enormous head" (Murdoch, *UN*, 220–21). The shift in lighting parallels the revelation that Hugo has read *The Silencer* and seen it not as a destructive lie or "touching up" of their conversation, but a refreshing new work, and this form of absolution (which is also a way for the novel to confront Hugo's original view that all paraphrase is a lie) exposes him to be just as absurd and imposing as he was in the dark. Earlier in the novel, after they left the cold-cure trials, Hugo invites Jake to live with him, but Jake rejects the offer on "some instinct of independence," a worry that "Hugo's personality could very easily swallow mine up completely" (Murdoch, *UN*, 61). Hugo's threatening otherness is reinforced at the end of the novel; even the revelation that he is paraphrased both in *The Silencer* and Jake's perception of him doesn't fundamentally change his position in, as it were, real life.

It is here that the relationship between Hugo and Jake gets physically expressed in a series of gestures. Hugo wants to leave the hospital, and Jake reluctantly decides to help; Murdoch spends several pages describing their escape through the ward:

> I slid out and Hugo followed, making a noise like a bear, a mixture of grunting and lumbering. I turned back and frowned and put my finger to my lips. Hugo nodded enthusiastically. I crouched down. . . . Then I turned to watch Hugo. He was hesitating. He obviously didn't know what to do with his boots, which he was carrying one in each hand. We each eyed each other across the gap and Hugo made an interrogatory movement. I replied with a gesture which indicated that I washed my hands of his predicament, and walked on to the

door of the ward. Then I turned back again, and nearly laughed out loud. Hugo had got his two boots gripped by their tongues between his teeth, and was negotiating the passage on hands and feet, his posterior rising mountainously into the air. . . . Hugo joined me by the door with the saliva dripping into the inside of his boots. I shook my head at him, and together we left Corelli III. (Murdoch, *UN*, 233)

For all the success Jake and Hugo have sneaking out of the hospital ward, the gestures they use to communicate are repeatedly and willfully misinterpreted. Hugo "nodded enthusiastically" when Jake frowns and tries to silence him; Hugo "makes an interrogatory movement" that Jake not only refuses to answer but thoroughly dismisses; when Hugo takes up the challenge and implements a strategy, Jake nearly laughs at him; and then once Hugo has successfully navigated his way out, Jake shakes his head. The misinterpretations have in common a rejection of the assessment of a predicament in favor of the predicament itself—the question of what in particular to do with one's shoes as a description of the difficulty involved in navigating a darkened corridor is replied to with a dismissal of the problem of navigation as a whole—and we could further generalize and say that Hugo's enthusiastic reply to Jake's frustration and anger restage for us his dispassionate, inquisitive relationship to expressions of emotion. That Hugo's enthusiasm comes across in the gesture while Jake's emotional signification is separated out from the description of his gesture (he doesn't "frowningly" put his finger to his lips) further indicates that whatever wrestling Jake does with the net that Hugo is always throwing over situations, Hugo's analytic approach incorporates gestures that actually express. Murdoch has already shown us that in an evaluative, gestural mode, action and tasks are productive of attention; what we see in Hugo is a form of attention breaking up into a series of parts—a dispassionate interest in the way actions are put together with signifiers of emotion (plausibly thought of as "tasks")—and as a result, the gesture that is produced carries a guileless emotion.

Portions of *The Silencer* are excerpted in the novel, and what

is most interesting about them is the way they begin to emphasize the pivotal role that paraphrase has in the production of
this kind of successful gesture. If Hugo can draw Jake into an
engagement with the net, this is because Hugo's gestures hold
action, tasks, and attention together; as this excerpt from *The Silencer* will show, the paraphrase of the facts of the world as their
value (the task of evaluation, figured in *Under the Net* as gesture)
occurs when another's language is appropriated into practical
life, where its moral significance is understood as that of an act,
performed on another person or on oneself.

The paraphrase of Hugo's conversation with Jake about the
infelicity of language reads like this. Jake (recast as "Tamarus")
says, "So you would cut all speech, except the very simplest, out
of human life altogether. To do this would be to take away our
very means of understanding ourselves and making life endur-
able" (Murdoch, *UN*, 81). Hugo (recast as "Annandine") replies:

> Why should life be made endurable? I know that nothing consoles
> and nothing justifies, except a story—but that doesn't stop all stories
> from being lies. Only the greatest men can speak and still be truth-
> ful. Any artist knows this obscurely; he knows that a theory is death,
> and that all expression is weighted with theory. Only the strongest
> can rise against that weight. For most of us, for almost all of us, truth
> can be attained, if at all, only in silence. It is in silence that the hu-
> man spirit touches the divine. (Murdoch, *UN*, 81)

Jake's first move is to think about the question of paraphrase as
a question of the endurability of life, to see it as the primary way
of dealing with the world. Hugo acknowledges both of the positions that Murdoch's assigns to value in her philosophy of ethics—the consolation of a just and loving gaze, and the imminent
value judgment that follows the application of criteria—and associates both with the story. Story is untrue because its language
is weighted with theory—"dryness" and "self-containedness"—
and so only silence connects humans with the divine—the rich
receding background, the preintentional "know how" that indicates to us that a view and our position inside of it is being

expressed. Rising against the weight of theory in *Under the Net* involves physically grappling with it, and this means incorporating within our most felicitous form of communication—"*actions don't lie*"—all of those ways of apprehending the world. It understands that the ethical value that actions bear is importantly without subjectivity, because attention is a product of actions and rules, and the best that can be hoped for is something like "nodding enthusiastically." There is an analogue earlier in the book, when Jake describes his friend Madge walking across a room: "She turned quietly to face me, with the quietness of somebody who knows that quietly is how they are turning" (Murdoch, *UN*, 173–74). The literal recursiveness of Madge's silent gesture is enough to align it with the ringed worlds that model her fact/ value distinctions. But in an important way, Madge animates those models: she shows us how they work, how they translate attention and criteria. She turns in an awareness of her relation to Jake only in terms of his physical otherness, the best possible transcendence from the consolation and judgment of the story she tells, contrived and mysterious, structured and loose.

Biographer Peter Conradi writes that just over a year after meeting Wittgenstein, Murdoch began what she described in her journals as a three-day "courtship" of his student Elizabeth Anscombe, a fascination Murdoch terms "almost frivolous. A vague sexual excitement." She contemplates Anscombe "with a sort of desire. Inclination to kiss her neck. (Something affected in all this.) I feel as light as a feather, can't even see myself as bloody or in danger or a menace to others." One of the things she earlier admires about Anscombe is her "ruthless authenticity," which "makes me feel more & more ashamed of the vague self-indulgent way in which I have been philosophizing," and so while she is worried about falling in love with a person who lacks "generosity, gentleness, douceur, tendresse, of all that for me lights up & gives grace to my attachments to people" Murdoch also sees these same qualities as dangerous, "especially in their corrupted form in me."[63]

There is much in this anecdote to bring us to some stark conclusions about Murdoch's personal representation of the fact/ value distinction, specifically the role that thinking plays as a compassionate moral action. Murdoch feels "light as a feather, can't even see myself as bloody or in danger or a menace to others," and it's surprising that she believes she *should* feel that way, that the visual attention to the other that is itself moralized should be subject to judgment when its gaze is just and loving. How is it, in other words, that we would find in her journals an admission that both positions are correct, that the gaze is a value and also an action? One answer is in her parenthesis, "(Something affected in all this.)" As we have seen, Murdoch often expresses the fact/value distinction as a parenthetical world, and here that world is affectedly paraphrased, a put-on of another voice. This affectedness embodies the threshold between fact and value; the description of her "inclination to kiss her neck" is filtered through affectedness into an inability to feel like a moral or physical danger to Anscombe.

The rationalizations that follow, in which Murdoch sees herself as a corrupted form of Anscombe's analytical philosophy, further cements the paraphrase's position as a hybridized approach to the world. In a passage that illuminates for us the final piece of her approach, her Wittgensteinian non-philosophy, Murdoch worries about what Wittgenstein himself will say if he learns from Anscombe that she and Murdoch are having an affair. Wittgenstein's "excessive attention to intellectual style—and *moral* style" masks a "real seriousness": "The style *is* a symptom." If the style was a totalizing vision for Murdoch before, a compounding of attention and criteria that we unpacked as a practice of paraphrase, then it shouldn't surprise us that a model of the distinction between fact and value would bring her to a similar conclusion. She adds a final parenthetical "(I see this in myself—relation of my "bad style" to my real badness)," the self-estrangement's connection between the style and the real illuminating Murdoch's own investment in paraphrase as the foundation for ethical practice.[64]

My earlier chapters argued that novels are theories of ref-

erence to intentional objects. The passage above shows us that
Murdoch essentially inverts that model: her theory of reference
is a theory of the novel. For if we allow Murdoch her assertion that Wittgensteinian moral style is a symptom, a form that
masks and contains the real seriousness beneath, then we should
be ready to admit that the contrivances of plots and characters are
indications of the constructedness of interiority and of the narratives that enclose it. As with Murdoch's earlier theorizations of
paraphrase, which soared into abstractions and thereby undercut
their own crystallization as particular images, this sneering at a
reference to seriousness returns us to the seriousness of her own
"badness." The fact that her assertions are reactions and tendencies rather than developed positions illustrates even more clearly
the practice and mechanism of the philosophical language of
reference, not as an account of how reference happens—Murdoch can't tell us how it happens—but as a demonstration of the
importance of accounting for reference as an embedded, situated
act. Murdoch only admits to "seeing" this same external "relation" inside herself, and yet, in so doing she reveals an instance
in which the referentiality of Wittgensteinian style could be said
to generate the seriousness of a self-referentiality. Her characterization of "badness" as both a style and a content interleaves
the genre (fiction), mode (realism), and problem (reference) that
concern this book. What is at stake in this moment for her is
nothing less than coherence of every imaginable form (literary,
ethical, psychological), and in her urgency to pin it down she
reveals the motivation that, for realist fiction and for the philosophy of reference, was there all along.

Notes

INTRODUCTION

1. Charles Dickens, *Great Expectations*, 3.

2. On self-reflexive pronouns, see Ian Rumfitt, "Frege's Theory of Predication: An Elaboration and Defense, with Some New Applications."

3. Dickens, *Great Expectations*, 7.

4. W. V. O. Quine, *Word and Object*, 1.

5. Dickens, *Great Expectations*, 7.

6. Charles Dickens, *Bleak House*, 6.

7. F. B. Perkins and Hippolyte Taine, *Charles Dickens: A Sketch of His Life and Works*, 221.

8. Dorothy Van Ghent, *The English Novel: Form and Function*, 125.

9. Ibid., 129.

10. Ibid., 133.

11. Peter Brooks, *Reading for the Plot*, 116–17.

12. Dickens, quoted in John Forster, *The Life of Charles Dickens*, 2:199.

13. One might also read this phrase colloquially, so that "there is a world to be done" means "there is much to be done." There may be "a world to do," or there may be "a *world* to do." All that is at stake in choosing a reading of this line is the question of whether or not Dickens is crediting the order of description with doing a *fictional* world, because he is unambiguous in his primary assertion: that the fate of popular literature (which includes both its representation of a fictional

world and its existence in the real world) depends on the "fanciful treatment" of things. The reader will find in the pages that follow that the question of whether or not an object being referred to is ontologically fictional is not central to the thrust of my argument about the problems of reference in novels. This example offers an early indication of why that might be, but there will be others.

14. Bertrand Russell, *Introduction to Mathematical Philosophy*, 178.

15. Ibid., 178.

16. Marga Reimer and Anne Bezuidenhout, *Descriptions and Beyond*, 3.

17. George Levine, *The Realistic Imagination: English Fiction from Frankenstein to Lady Chatterley*, 4.

18. Catherine Gallagher, "The Failure of Realism: *Felix Holt*," 380; 384.

19. Elaine Freedgood, *The Ideas in Things: Fugitive Meaning and the Victorian Novel*, 141.

20. Ibid., 148.

21. Caroline Levine, *Forms: Whole, Rhythm, Hierarchy, Network*, 86.

22. Robert Brandom, *Articulating Reasons*, 41.

23. George Gissing, *Charles Dickens: A Critical Study*, 60.

24. Elaine Scarry, *Dreaming by the Book*, 28.

25. Ibid., 12.

26. Ibid., 66; Ludwig Wittgenstein, *Culture and Value*, 24e.

27. Scarry, *Dreaming*, 26.

28. John Locke, *An Essay Concerning Human Understanding*, 186.

29. Elizabeth Anscombe, "The Intentionality of Sensation," 5.

30. Elizabeth Anscombe, "Substance," 41.

31. Ibid., 42.

32. Anscombe, "Under a Description," 208–9.

33. Sean D. Kelly, *The Relevance of Phenomenology to the Philosophy of Language and Mind*, 3.

34. Sean D. Kelly, "Seeing Things in Merleau-Ponty," 79.

35. Ibid., 80; Merleau-Ponty, *The Phenomenology of Perception*, 7, 13, 6.

36. Merleau-Ponty, *Phenomenology of Perception*, 361, 352.

37. I take this phrasing from Martha Nussbaum, *Upheavals of Thought*, 1.

38. Sianne Ngai, *Ugly Feelings*, 30.

39. I. A. Richards, *Practical Criticism: A Study of Literary Judgment*, 209.

40. Ngai, *Ugly Feelings*, 22.

41. Deidre Lynch, *The Economy of Character*, 205.

42. Alex Woloch, *The One vs. the Many*, 7.

43. Ibid., 29.

44. Bill Brown, *A Sense of Things*, 3.

45. Ibid.

46. Ibid., 11.

47. Ibid., 25.

48. Charles Altieri, "The Sensuous Dimension of Literary Experience," 84.

49. Ibid., 83.

50. Anscombe, "Substance," 42.

51. Ibid., 43.

52. Altieri, "The Sensuous Dimension," 84.

53. John Searle, "On the Logical Status of Fictional Discourse," 297.

54. Monroe C. Beardsley, "An Aesthetic Definition of Art," 59.

55. Jerrold Levinson, "What a Musical Work Is," 84.

56. Jack W. Meiland, "Originals, Copies, and Aesthetic Value," 380.

57. Richard Wollheim, "On Pictorial Representation," 400.

58. I have found the following source especially useful for its interpretation of the impact of Millianism on the split between Quine and Russell, a genealogy that is so embedded into subsequent discussions of reference that it rarely gets its own treatment: Marga Reimer, "Reference," in *The Stanford Encyclopedia of Philosophy*, online at http://plato.stanford.edu/entries/reference/.

59. Bertrand Russell, *Introduction to Mathematical Philosophy* (New York: Routledge, 1993), 168.

60. P. F. Strawson, "On Referring."

61. Gareth Evans, *The Varieties of Reference*, 106.

62. John Searle, *Intentionality*.

63. Saul Kripke, *Naming and Necessity*.

64. W. V. O. Quine, *Ontological Relativity and Other Essays*.

65. Donald Davidson, "Epistemology Externalized."

66. Kelly, *Relevance of Phenomenology*, 17.

CHAPTER ONE

1. Ioan M. Williams, *Meredith: The Critical Heritage*, 1. Meredith was never a successful novelist, critically or commercially; his reputation declined as he was more widely read, and obituary reassessments actually suggested that he might have been more fondly remembered—and might not have been flatly refused a place at Westminster Abbey—had he only died twenty-five years earlier. Virginia Woolf is right to claim

that Meredith despised and desired the public in turns, and that once he failed to snag it, he "wrecked his failure upon the public by a succession, gradually increasing in intensity, of angularities, obscurities, and affections which no writer whose patron was his equal and friend would have thought it necessary to inflict" (Woolf, "The Patron and the Crocus," 207). By Meredith's centennial, E. M. Forster could write with confidence that Meredith "now lies in the trough" (Forster, *Aspects of the Novel*, 49). For more on the critical reception of Meredith's novels (however shot through with recuperative praise), see L. T. Hergenhan, "Meredith's Attempts to Win Popularity: Contemporary Reactions," and "Meredith Achieves Recognition: The Reception of *Beauchamp's Career* and *The Egoist*"; Siegfried Sassoon, *Meredith*.

2. Philippe Hamon, in "Rhetorical Status of the Descriptive," observes that, for theoretical discussions of the descriptive, the impossibility of holding the reader's reactions to the descriptive—of managing his drift from detail to detail—gives the reader the "choice of absenting himself from the text, of 'skipping' it . . . no longer ruled by the very act of reading" (10). He replies directly to Valéry's claim that there is "Nothing more natural, nothing more *true*, than this vagrancy" (quoted in Hamon, "Rhetorical Status," 10), arguing that the detail that "suspends the momentum of reading" also "requests a 'translation' as to its meaning, its function in the work; it calls upon and interrogates the reader whom it transforms into an interpreter; it is simultaneously asyndeton and anaphora" (11). Of course, this is the position Meredith's critics take when they suggest that his difficulty is somehow good for us.

3. Oscar Wilde, "The Decay of Lying," in *The Complete Works of Oscar Wilde*, 976.

4. Thus we often see a too-easy collapse in criticism of Meredith's novels of the ideological into structure and plot. For an example of this in criticism on *The Egoist*, see Jonathan Smith, "'The Cock of Lordly Plume': Sexual Selection and *The Egoist*"; Natalie Cole Michta, "The Legitimate Self in George Meredith's *Evan Harrington*"; Maaja A. Stewart, "The Country House Ideals in Meredith's *The Egoist*"; Christopher Morris, "Richard Feveral and the Fictional Lineage of Desire", and "Hands Around: Image and Theme in *The Egoist*"; Jean Sudrann, "'The Linked Eye and Mind': A Concept of Action in the Novels of George Meredith."

5. I borrow this definition of the term *accommodation* from David Lewis, for whom it is a repair strategy, a readjustment of the context of

a conversation in order to accept utterances that would not make sense otherwise; see his "Scorekeeping in a Language Game."

6. Steven Knapp and Walter Benn Michaels, "Against Theory."

7. W. K. Wimsatt and Monroe C. Beardsley, "The Intentional Fallacy," 1015.

8. Paul de Man, "Form and Intent in the American New Criticism," 29.

9. Michel Foucault, *The Archaeology of Knowledge*, 125.

10. Ludwig Wittgenstein, *Philosophical Investigations*, §635–36. Stanley Cavell looks to the moment just after action happens to describe the process by which (or, as he would have it, the criteria under which) an act gives its intention: "It is not merely that to know *I* have in fact *done* what I intended (or hoped, or promised . . .), I have to look to see *whether* it is done; it is also, and crucially, that I have to know that *that* circumstance *is* (counts as) *what* I did" (Cavell, *The Claim of Reason*, 108). Rather than simply saying that we grasp some proposition or other to interpret the intention that discharges the act, Wittgenstein is saying that the act itself holds the circumstances under which it is intentional.

11. Candace Vogler, *Reasonably Vicious*, 210. For an illuminating contrast between the analyses of causal chains in Anscombe's and Donald Davidson's work, see Vogler's "Anscombe on Practical Inference."

12. Wittgenstein, *Philosophical Investigations*, §374.

13. Ibid., §66.

14. Krishna Jain, *Description in Philosophy*, 21.

15. George Meredith, *The Egoist*, 32; hereafter cited parenthetically by *E* and page number.

16. Elizabeth Anscombe, "On the Grammar of 'Enjoy,'" 96. J. L. Austin's "Three Ways of Spilling Ink," in which he teases out "acting *intentionally*, and acting *deliberately*, or *on purpose*," turns on a remarkably similar example: "Again, we ask this young man who is paying attentions to our daughter to declare his intentions. What are his intentions? Are his intentions honorable? Here, would it make any difference if we asked him what was the purpose of these attentions, whether he had some purpose in view, whether he is doing these things on purpose or for a purpose? This makes his conduct seem more calculated, frames him as an adventurer or seducer. Instead of asking him to clarify the position, perhaps to himself as well as to us, are we not now asking him to divulge a guilty secret?" (430).

17. Anscombe, "On the Grammar of 'Enjoy,'" 96.

18. One of Anscombe's core insights is that the structure of intentional action can be separated from its content and elucidated by the question "Why are you *A*-ing?" She posits that if we ask agents why they are doing this or that particular thing at various stages of an intentional action, the calculative form that underlies the representations of that action will be revealed in their parts and wholes, means and ends. According to Vogler, "The genius of the 'Why?' question as a way of eliciting this structure is, perhaps, that it locates the structure in the action unambiguously first and foremost, and so defeats the temptation to hunt for it first in the content of a man's occurrent thoughts before he makes a move" (Vogler, *Reasonably Vicious*, 128–29).

19. V. S. Pritchett, *George Meredith and English Comedy*, 43. Elsewhere Pritchett reminds us that Meredith himself thought of the leap into fantasy as both expedient and condescending. In *Beauchamp's Career*, for example, Miss Halkett says to Beauchamp, "I know you wouldn't talk down to me but the use of imagery makes me feel that I am addressed as a primitive intelligence," to which he replies, "That's the fault of my trying at condensation, as the hieroglyphists put an animal for a paragraph. I am incorrigible, you see" (quoted in Pritchett, *George Meredith*, 50).

20. George Meredith, *The Amazing Marriage*, 122–23.

21. Pritchett, *George Meredith*, 46.

22. Meredith, *Amazing Marriage*, 69.

23. Meredith's descriptions are frequently said to stack up without developing. See Randall Craig, "Promising Marriage: *The Egoist*, Don Juan, and the Problem of Language"; and Daniel Smirlock, "Rough Truth: Synecdoche and Interpretation in *The Egoist*." Allon White, in *The Uses of Obscurity*, argues that "Meredith's work is everywhere marked by the pressure of an excessive presence . . . as though everything had to be revealed all at once and narrative time were merely a series of total, arresting revelations. The pressure of exposure is intense, and it reveals itself as a condensed consciousness of the moment at the expense of continuity. Both at the general level of narrative sequence and at the level of syntax, Meredith compresses things so intensely that continuous movement is often lost in the flash of vivid and discrete sparks of consciousness" (88). I think White is right to recast these descriptions as "revelations," but consciousness and continuity seem to me arbitrary—even counterfactual—rivals.

24. For more on Clara's scenes of deliberation as self-estrangement, see J. Hillis Miller, "'Herself Against Herself': The Clarification of Clara Middleton"; and Carolyn Williams, "Unbroken Patternes: Gender, Culture, and Voice in *The Egoist*."

25. Unresolved psychological portraits in Meredith generate a great deal of interest, since intricate characterization and reported interior monologues dominate much of his fiction. Critics tend to project any psychological unknowns into character behavior or thematic and stylistic systems. See Robert S. Baker, "Sir Willoughby Patterne's 'Inner Temple': Psychology and 'Sentimentalism' in *The Egoist*."

26. G. E. M. Anscombe, *Intention*, 4. Anscombe positions herself against W. V. O. Quine, who argues for the "baselessness of intentional idioms and the emptiness of a science of intention," but she understands why he rejects them. Quine's view is that "to accept intentional usage at face value is . . . to postulate translation relations as somehow objectively valid though indeterminate in principle relative to the totality of speech dispositions" (Quine, *Word and Object*, 221). This sounds rather a lot like Anscombe's position: "We need a more fruitful line of enquiry than that of considering the verbal expression of intention, or of trying to consider what it is an expression of. For if we consider just the verbal expression of intention, we arrive only at its being a—queer—species of prediction; and if we try to look for what it is an expression of, we are likely to find ourselves in one or other of several dead ends. E.g.: psychological jargon about 'drives' and 'sets'; reduction of intention to a species of desire, i.e., a kind of emotion; or irreducible intuition of the meaning of 'I intend'" (6). Naturally, "translation relations" work both ways, and Meredith's own statement of intention will be as problematic a theory of practice as his critics' perpetually regressing attacks. What matters in this case is that Meredith's work is as eager to expose the machinery of intention as its effects, and learning to read one and not the other is, it seems to me, his primary narrative engine.

27. Anscombe explores the difference between "grounds" and "causes" for acting in "Under a Description," and "A Reply to Mr. C. S. Lewis's Argument that 'Naturalism' Is Self-Refuting."

28. Elizabeth Anscombe, "The First Person," 28. See also Brian J. Garrett, "Anscombe and the First Person." For a look at the challenges associated with Anscombe's circumscription of the first person—particularly her correlative treatment of self-consciousness—see Gareth Evans, *The Varieties of Reference*, 205–57.

29. Anscombe, "First Person," 32.

30. Anscombe, *Intention*, 46. A symposium on "The Individuation of Action" revisited Anscombe's work on "swallowing up." See Alvin I. Goldman, "The Individuation of Actions"; Judith Jarvis Thompson, "Individuating Actions"; and Irving Thalberg, "Singling Out Actions: Their Properties and Components," in the *Journal of Philosophy* 68, no. 20 (1971): 761–87. See also Julia Annas, "Davidson and Anscombe on 'the Same Action.'"

31. Gary J. Handwerk, "Linguistic Blindness and Ironic Vision in *The Egoist*," 176.

CHAPTER TWO

1. This formulation recalls that in George Gissing's *The Odd Women* (1893):

> "But—" the girl hesitated—"don't you approve of any one marrying?"
>
> "Oh, I'm not so severe! But do you know that there are half a million more women than men in this happy country of ours?"
>
> "Half a million!"
>
> Her naive alarm again excited Rhoda to laughter.
>
> "Something like that, they say. So many odd women—no making a pair with them. The pessimists call them useless, lost, futile lives. I, naturally—being one of them myself—take another view. I look upon them as a great reserve. When one woman vanishes in matrimony, the reserve offers a substitute for the world's work. True, they are not all trained yet—far from it. I want to help in that—to train the reserve." (George Gissing, *The Odd Women*, 103–4)

2. William Makepeace Thackeray, *The Memoirs of Barry Lyndon, Esq.*, ed. Andrew Sanders (Oxford: Oxford University Press, 1999), 206; hereafter cited parenthetically as *BL*, and page number.

3. Maurice Merleau-Ponty, *The Phenomenology of Perception*, trans. Colin Smith (New York: Routledge, 2003), 100.

4. For a further exploration of mediational epistemology as it intersects with "ordinary coping" in Merleau-Ponty, see Charles Taylor, "Merleau-Ponty and the Epistemological Picture."

5. I borrow this perhaps unfair characterization of phenomenological accounts of perception from Sean Dorrance Kelly's analysis of the intersections between theories of perception in Merleau-Ponty and Edmund Husserl; see "Seeing Things in Merleau-Ponty."

6. James Fitzjames Stephen, review of *Barry Lyndon*, by William Makepeace Thackeray, 27.

7. Merleau-Ponty, *Phenomenology of Perception*, 100.

8. William Makepeace Thackeray, *The Letters and Private Papers of William Makepeace Thackeray*, 2:29–30.

9. Richard Bedingfield, "Recollections of Thackeray: Prologue," *Cassell's Magazine*, September 2, 1870, 14.

10. Anthony Trollope, *Thackeray*, 72.

11. Anne Thackeray Ritchie, introduction to *The Memoirs of Barry Lyndon, Esq.*, xxxiii–xxxiv.

12. William Makepeace Thackeray, *Vanity Fair*, ed. John Sutherland (Oxford: Oxford University Press, 1983), 229.

13. William Makepeace Thackeray, *The Book of Snobs* (Köln: Könemann, 1999), 23.

14. William Makepeace Thackeray, *Pendennis* (London: J. M. Dent, 1910), 337.

15. William Makepeace Thackeray, "Autour de mon chapeau," in *The Roundabout Papers* (New York: Houghton, Mifflin, 1889), 280.

16. Ibid.

17. Bertrand Russell, *The Philosophy of Logical Atomism* (New York: Open Court, 1985), 113.

18. Merleau-Ponty, *Phenomenology of Perception*, 103–4.

19. Merleau-Ponty, *Phenomenology of Perception*, 120.

20. Robert A. Colby, "Barry Lyndon and the Irish Hero," 112.

21. The narrative influence of Freeny's story is well documented in Colby, (ibid., 119–120) and in chapter 4 of *Barry Lyndon* itself. Three issues of *Notes and Queries* follow up the search for information about the real Captain James Freeney. *Notes and Queries* (January–March, 1912), 50, 156, 234.

22. William Makepeace Thackeray, *The Irish Sketch Book*, 156.

23. Henry Fielding, *Jonathan Wild*, 9.

24. Thackeray, *Irish Sketch Book*, 156.

25. Ibid., 166.

26. My reading of egocentric space is derived from Gareth Evans, *The Varieties of Reference*, 157.

27. The formulation of absence as positive presence is derived from Maurice Merleau-Ponty, *Husserl at the Limits of Phenomenology*, ed. Leonard Lawlor and Bettina Bergo (Evanston, IL: Northwestern University Press, 2002), 44.

28. Merleau-Ponty, *Phenomenology of Perception*, 105; Evans, *Varieties of Reference*, 153–54.

29. Merleau-Ponty, *Phenomenology of Perception*, 117.

30. Ibid.

31. Evans takes his conception of the sufficient conditions for being able to distinguish an object from all other things from Peter Strawson's account in "Identifying Reference."

32. Evans, *Varieties of Reference*, 151.

33. Ibid., 152.

34. Ibid., 43.

35. Ibid., 89.

36. Ibid., 108.

37. Michael Dummett, *Frege* (Cambridge, MA: Harvard University Press, 1981), 227.

38. For a useful account of the stakes, structure, and logics of Evans's argument, see R. M. Sainsbury, review of *The Varieties of Reference*, by Gareth Evans.

39. Bertrand Russell, *Introduction to Mathematical Philosophy* (New York: Routledge, 1993), 169–70.

40. Ritchie, introduction to *The Memoirs of Barry Lyndon*, xxxv–xxxvi.

41. Evans, *Varieties of Reference*, 17.

42. Sean Dorrance Kelly, *The Relevance of Phenomenology to the Philosophy of Language and Mind*, 67.

CHAPTER THREE

1. Gareth Evans, *The Varieties of Reference*, vi. Hereafter cited parenthetically as Evans, *VR*, and page number.

2. Stephen Schiffer, review of *The Varieties of Reference* by Gareth Evans, 33.

3. Elizabeth Gaskell, *Cranford*, 3. Hereafter cited parenthetically by page number.

4. Andrew H. Miller, "The Fragments and Small Opportunities of *Cranford*," 92.

5. Bill Brown, *A Sense of Things*, 6.

6. Ibid., 49.

7. Ibid., 50.

8. John Plotz, *Portable Property: Victorian Culture on the Move*, 1.

9. Ibid., 10.

10. Ibid., 11.

11. Christina Lupton, "Theorizing Surfaces and Depths: Gaskell's *Cranford*," 237.

12. Ibid., 236.

13. Ibid., 244.

14. Brown, *Sense of Things*, 5.

15. J. Hillis Miller, *Reading Narrative*, 165.

CHAPTER FOUR

1. Iris Murdoch, "The Idea of Perfection," 13.

2. Martha Nussbaum, "Faint with Secret Knowledge: Love and Vision in Murdoch's *The Black Prince*; Peter Lamarque, "Truth and Art in Iris Murdoch's *The Black Prince*." For a deeper and more capacious theorization of translation as a moral act, see Valeria Wagner, *Bound to Act*.

3. Peter Conradi, *Iris Murdoch: A Life*, 263. As of this writing, Murdoch's diaries remain unpublished; all entries quoted from her diaries are found in Conradi's work. For a literary critical approach to much of the biographical content, see Conradi's *The Saint and the Artist*.

4. Conradi, *Iris Murdoch*, 266.

5. Iris Murdoch, *Nuns and Soldiers*, 3.

6. Murdoch, "Idea of Perfection," 15.

7. Iris Murdoch, *Metaphysics as a Guide to Morals*, 280.

8. Iris Murdoch, *Under the Net*, 238; hereafter cited parenthetically as Murdoch, *UN*, and page number.

9. Iris Murdoch, interview by Michael O. Bellamy, 132.

10. Murdoch, *Metaphysics*, 283.

11. Iris Murdoch, "Literature and Philosophy: A Conversation with Bryan Magee," 7.

12. Murdoch, interview by Bellamy, 138.

13. Murdoch, *Metaphysics*, 25–26.

14. For an illuminating and, I think, sympathetic take on the translation of meaning or signification in language as "transcoding," see Algirdas Julien Greimas and Paul Ricoeur, "On Narrativity."

15. Iris Murdoch, "Vision and Choice in Morality," 40–41. See also Lawrence A. Blum, "Iris Murdoch and the Domain of the Moral"; and E. W. Denham, "Envisioning the Good: Iris Murdoch's Moral Psychology."

16. Iris Murdoch, "The Sublime and the Good," 43.

17. Frank Kermode, "The House of Fiction," 63–64.

18. Iris Murdoch, "The Sublime and the Beautiful Revisited," 262.

On Murdoch's literary critical practice, see George Watson, "Iris Murdoch and the Net of Theory." For more on the structure of language, the structure of experience, and the structure of the novel (and George Eliot), see William Charlton, "Is Philosophy a Form of Literature?" and D. W. Theobald, "Philosophy and Fiction."

19. Murdoch, interview by Bellamy, 130. Murdoch's valorization of the novel over high Modernist poetry (whose language is seen as originating in historical fact and producing exteriorization), her anti-existentialism and value of ordinary language, and her concerns over the social determinism of interiority are more or less traceable to the Oxbridge intellectual climate of the 1950s and 1960s. All of which would indicate that, for Murdoch, reclaiming subjectivity necessitates reclaiming a novelistic narrative form, rendering the opposition between fact and value less a philosophical system than a theory of the novel.

20. Murdoch, "Idea of Perfection," 16–17.

21. Ibid., 17.

22. Ibid., 33.

23. Ibid., 31.

24. Ibid., 37.

25. Simone Weil, *Gravity and Grace*, 118.

26. Murdoch, "Idea of Perfection," 38.

27. Stanley Cavell, *The Claim of Reason*, 13.

28. Iris Murdoch, "Against Dryness," 16.

29. Ibid.

30. Ibid., 17.

31. Ibid., 20. For a fuller exploration of the picture theory and "background," see Ann Culley, "Theory and Practice: Characterization in the Novels of Iris Murdoch." For a specific application to *Under the Net*, see R. L. Widmann, "Murdoch's *Under the Net*: Theory and Practice of Fiction."

32. Ibid., 19.

33. Ibid.

34. John Searle, *Intentionality*, 141.

35. David Sosa, "Checking Searle's Background," 109–10.

36. John Searle, "The Logical Status of Fictional Discourse," 319.

37. Iris Murdoch, *The Red and the Green*, 3.

38. Searle, "Logical Status," 324.

39. Ibid.

40. Ibid., 325.

41. Ibid., 330.

42. Ibid. See also Kenneth Walton, *Mimesis as Make-Believe*; and Anthony Everett, "Pretense, Existence, and Fictional Objects."

43. Ibid., 331.

44. Stanley Fish, "How to Do Things with Austin and Searle: Speech Act Theory and Literary Criticism," 1016. See also Pierre Bourdieu, *Homo Academicus*.

45. Fish, "How to Do Things," 1022.

46. Murdoch, *Metaphysics*, 485.

47. Saul Kripke, *Wittgenstein on Rules and Private Language*, 102.

48. Murdoch, *Metaphysics*, 285.

49. Murdoch, "Dryness," 19.

50. Murdoch, *Metaphysics*, 278.

51. Ibid., 279. For more on the danger of mimicking Wittgenstein while talking about Wittgenstein, see Brett Bourbon, "Wittgenstein's Preface."

52. Ibid., 279.

53. Murdoch, interview by Bellamy, 137.

54. Ludwig Wittgenstein, *Tractatus Logico-Philosophicus*, §6.341.

55. Murdoch, quoted in Kermode, "House of Fiction," 65.

56. Wittgenstein, *Tractatus*, §4.04.

57. Ibid., §6.342.

58. Iris Murdoch, interview by S. B. Sagare, 702.

59. L. R. Leavis, "The Anti-Artist: The Case of Iris Murdoch," 139.

60. Ludwig Wittgenstein, *Culture and Value*, 73.

61. Conradi, *Iris Murdoch*, 381.

62. For the position that Murdoch's rendering of Jake's intellectual crisis is too cavalier, see Malcolm Bradbury, "Iris Murdoch's *Under the Net*." The dialogue lightens the tone and quickens the pace of the novel, but it also expels Jake from his own mind in a way that enables his self-reflexivity; see Steven G. Kellman, "Raising the Net: Iris Murdoch and the Tradition of the Self-Begetting Novel"; and David J. Gordon, "Iris Murdoch's Comedies of Unselfing." For a characterization of *Under the Net* as Murdoch's best—because least serious—novel, see Harold Bloom, "Introduction," 1–7.

63. Conradi, *Iris Murdoch*, 284.

64. Ibid., 285.

Bibliography

Altieri, Charles. "The Sensuous Dimension of Literary Experience." *New Literary History* 38, no. 1 (2007): 71–98.

Alvarez, Maria. "Agents, Actions, and Reasons." *Philosophical Books* 46, no. 1 (2005): 45–58.

Annas, Julia. "Davidson and Anscombe on 'the Same Action.'" *Mind* 85, no. 338 (1976): 251–57.

Anscombe, G. E. M. "The First Person." In *Metaphysics*, 21–36.

———. *Intention.* Cambridge, MA: Harvard University Press, 1957.

———. "The Intentionality of Sensation." In *Metaphysics*, 3–20.

———. *Metaphysics and the Philosophy of Mind.* Oxford: Basil Blackwell, 1981.

———. "On the Grammar of 'Enjoy.'" In *Metaphysics*, 94–102.

———. "Pretending." *Proceedings of the Aristotelian Society Supplement* 32 (1958): 279–94.

———. "A Reply to Mr. C. S. Lewis's Argument That 'Naturalism' Is Self-Refuting." In *Metaphysics*, 224–32.

———. "Substance." In *Metaphysics*, 37–43.

———. "Under a Description." In *Metaphysics*, 208–19.

Auerbach, Erich. *Mimesis: The Representation of Reality in Western Literature.* Translated by Willard R. Trask. Princeton, NJ: Princeton University Press, 1953.

Austin, J. L. "Pretending." *Proceedings of the Aristotelian Society Supplement* 32 (1958): 261–78.

―――. "Three Ways of Spilling Ink." *Philosophical Review* 75, no. 4 (1966): 427–40.

Baker, Robert S. "Sir Willoughby Patterne's 'Inner Temple': Psychology and 'Sentimentalism' in *The Egoist*." *Texas Studies in Literature and Language* 14, no. 4 (1975): 691–703.

Barrett, Cyril. "Not Exactly Pretending." *Philosophy* 44, no. 170 (1969): 331–38.

Barthes, Roland. *The Rustle of Language*. Translated by Richard Howard. New York: Hill and Wang, 1986.

Beardsley, Monroe C. "An Aesthetic Definition of Art." In Lamarque and Olsen, *Aesthetics and the Philosophy of Art*, 55–62..

Bedingfield, Richard. "Recollections of Thackeray: Prologue." *Cassell's Magazine* (September 2, 1870): 12–14.

Bell, Robert. Review of *Vanity Fair* by William Makepeace Thackeray. *Fraser's Magazine* 38 (1848): 321.

Benjamin, Lewis Saul. *William Makepeace Thackeray*. London: John Lane, 1910.

Bloom, Harold. "Introduction." In *Modern Critical Views: Iris Murdoch*, 1–7, edited by Harold Bloom. New York: Chelsea House, 1986.

Blum, Lawrence A. "Iris Murdoch and the Domain of the Moral." *Philosophical Studies* 50, no. 3 (1986): 343–67.

Bourbon, Brett. "Wittgenstein's Preface." *Philosophy and Literature* 29 (2005): 428–43.

Bourdieu, Pierre. *Homo Academicus*. Translated by Peter Collier. Stanford, CA: Stanford University Press, 1988.

―――. *Outline of a Theory of Practice*. Translated by Richard Nice. New York: Cambridge University Press, 1977.

Bradbury, Malcolm. "Iris Murdoch's *Under the Net*." *Critical Quarterly* 4, no. 1 (1962): 47–54.

Brandom, Robert. *Articulating Reasons*. Cambridge, MA: Harvard University Press, 2000.

―――. *Making It Explicit: Reasoning, Representing, and Discursive Commitment*. Cambridge, MA: Harvard University Press, 1994.

Bratman, Michael. "Intention and Means-End Reasoning." *Philosophical Review* 90, no. 2 (1981): 252–65.

Brooks, Peter. *The Novel of Worldliness*. Princeton, NJ: Princeton University Press, 1969.

―――. *Reading for the Plot*. Cambridge, MA: Harvard University Press, 1984.

Brown, Bill. *A Sense of Things.* Chicago: University of Chicago Press, 2003.

Carman, Taylor, and Mark B. N. Hansen, eds. *The Cambridge Companion to Merleau-Ponty.* New York: Cambridge University Press, 2005.

Catalano, Joseph S. "Successfully Lying to Oneself: A Sartrean Perspective." *Philosophy and Phenomenological Research* 50, no. 4 (1990): 673–93.

Cavell, Stanley. *The Claim of Reason.* New York: Oxford, 1979.

Cebik, L. B. "The World Is Not a Novel." *Philosophy and Literature* 16, no. 1 (1992): 68–87.

Charlton, William. "Is Philosophy a Form of Literature?" *British Journal of Aesthetics* 14, no. 1 (1974): 3–16.

Chesterton, G. K. "The Method of Allusive Irrelevancy." In *Thackeray: A Collection of Critical Essays*, edited by Alexander Welsh, 15–19. Englewood, NJ: Prentice-Hall, 1968.

Colby, Robert A. "Barry Lyndon and the Irish Hero." *Nineteenth-Century Fiction* 21, no. 2 (1966): 109–30.

Colyvan, Mark. "Russell on Metaphysical Vagueness." *Principia* 5, nos. 1–2 (2001): 87–98.

Conolly, Oliver. "Pleasure and Pain in Literature." *Philosophy and Literature* 29 (2005): 305–20.

Conradi, Peter. *Iris Murdoch: A Life.* New York: W. W. Norton, 2001.

———. *The Saint and the Artist.* New York: Harper Collins, 1989.

Craig, Randall. "Promising Marriage: *The Egoist*, Don Juan, and the Problem of Language." *ELH* 56, no. 4 (1989): 897–921.

Culley, Ann. "Theory and Practice: Characterization in the Novels of Iris Murdoch." *Modern Fiction Studies* 15, no. 3 (1969): 335–45.

Currie, Gregory. "Fictional Names." *Australian Journal of Philosophy* 66, no. 4 (1988): 471–88.

Davidson, Donald. "Epistemology Externalized." *Dialectica* 45, nos. 2–3 (1991): 191–202.

———. "Truth and Meaning." *Synthese* 17 (1967): 304–23.

de Man, Paul. *Blindness and Insight: Essays in the Rhetoric of Contemporary Criticism.* Minneapolis: University of Minnesota Press, 1983.

———. *The Rhetoric of Romanticism.* New York: Columbia University Press, 1984.

Denham, E. W. "Envisioning the Good: Iris Murdoch's Moral Psychology." *Modern Fiction Studies* 47, no. 3 (2001): 602–29.

Dickens, Charles. *Great Expectations.* New York: Penguin, 1996.

Donnellan, Keith S. "Reference and Definite Descriptions." *Philosophical Review* 75, no. 3 (1966): 281–304.

Dretske, Fred I. "Causal Theories of Reference." *Journal of Philosophy* 74, no. 10 (1977): 621–25.

Dreyfus, Hubert, and Sean D. Kelly, "Heterophenomenology: Heavy-handed sleight-of-hand." *Phenomenology and Cognitive Sciences* 6, nos. 1–2 (2007): 45–55.

———, and Charles Spinosa. "Coping with Things-in-themselves: A Practice-Based Phenomenological Argument for Realism." *Inquiry* 42, no. 1 (1999): 42–78.

Dummett, Michael. *Frege.* Cambridge, MA: Harvard University Press, 1981.

———. "Nominalism." *Philosophical Review* 65, no. 4 (1956): 491–505.

———. "Wang's Paradox." *Synthese* 30 (1975): 301–24.

———. "What Is a Theory of Meaning?" In *Mind and Language,* edited by S. D. Guttenplan, 97–138. Oxford: Clarendon, 1975.

Eco, Umberto. "Meaning and Denotation." *Synthese* 73 (1987): 549–68.

Elster, Jon. *Alchemies of the Mind.* New York: Cambridge University Press, 1999.

———. *Ulysses Unbound.* New York: Cambridge University Press, 2000.

Evans, Gareth. *The Varieties of Reference.* New York: Oxford University Press, 1982.

Everett, Anthony. "Pretense, Existence, and Fictional Objects." *Philosophy and Phenomenological Research* 74, no. 1 (2007): 56–80.

Fielding, Henry. *Jonathan Wild.* New York: Oxford University Press, 2003.

Fine, Kit. "Vagueness, Truth, and Logic." *Synthese* 30 (1975): 265–300.

Fish, Stanley. "How to Do Things with Austin and Searle: Speech Act Theory and Literary Criticism." *MLN* 91, no. 5 (1976): 983–1025.

Fletcher, Robert P. "The Dandy and the Fogy: Thackeray and Aesthetics/Ethics of the Literary Pragmatist." *ELH* 58, no. 2 (1991): 383–404.

———. "'Proving a thing even while you contradict it': Fictions, Beliefs, and Legitimation in *The Memoirs of Barry Lyndon, Esq.*" *Studies in the Novel* 27, no. 4 (1995): 493–514.

Forster, E. M. *Aspects of the Novel.* New York: Harvest, 1927.

Forster, John. *The Life of Charles Dickens, Volume II.* London: Chapman and Hall, 1870.

————. Review of *Vanity Fair* by William Makepeace Thackeray. *Examiner* (22 July, 1848): 57.

Foucault, Michel. *The Archaeology of Knowledge.* Translated by A. M. Sheridan Smith. New York: Pantheon, 1972.

Freedgood, Elaine. *The Ideas in Things: Fugitive Meaning and the Victorian Novel.* Chicago: University of Chicago Press, 2006.

Gallagher, Catherine. "The Failure of Realism: *Felix Holt,*" *Nineteenth-Century Fiction* 35, no. 3 (1980): 372–84.

————. "George Eliot: Immanent Victorian." *Representations* 90 (2005): 61–74.

García-Carpintero, Manuel. "Vagueness and Indirect Discourse." *Philosophical Issues* 10, no. 1 (2000): 258–343.

Garrett, Brian J. "Anscombe and the First Person." *Critica* 26, no. 78 (1994): 97–113.

Gaskell, Elizabeth. *Cranford.* Edited by Dinah Birch. New York: Oxford University Press, 2008.

Gendler, Tamar Szabó. "The Puzzle of Imaginative Resistence." *Journal of Philosophy* 97, no. 2 (2000): 55–81.

Genette, Gérard. "Fictional Narrative, Factual Narrative." Translated by Nitsa Ben-Ari and Brian McHale. *Poetics Today* 11, no. 4 (1990): 755–74.

Gissing, George. *Charles Dickens: A Critical Study.* Glasgow: Blackie and Son, 1898.

————. *The Odd Women.* London: Lawrence and Bullen, 1893.

Goldman, Alvin I. "The Individuation of Action." *Journal of Philosophy* 68, no. 20 (1971): 761–74.

Goodman, Nelson. "Routes of Reference." *Critical Inquiry* 8, no. 1 (1981): 121–32.

————. "Some Reflections on the Theory of Systems." *Philosophy and Phenomenological Research* 9, no. 3 (1949): 620–26.

————. "Words, Works, Worlds." *Erkenntnis* 9 (1975): 57–73.

Gordon, David J. "Iris Murdoch's Comedies of Unselfing." *Twentieth-Century Literature* 36, no. 2 (1990): 115–36.

Greimas, Algirdas Julien, and Paul Ricoeur. "On Narrativity." Translated by Paul Perron and Frank Collins. *New Literary History* 20, no. 3 (1989): 551–62.

Hamon, Philippe. "Rhetorical Status of the Descriptive." Translated by Patricia Baudoin. *Yale French Studies* 61 (1981): 1–26.

Handwerk, Gary J. "Linguistic Blindness and Ironic Vision in *The Egoist.*" *Nineteenth-Century Fiction* 39, no. 2 (1984): 163–85.

Hansen, Mark B. N. "Wearable Space." *Configurations* 10 (2002): 321–70.

Harden, Edgar F. "The Discipline and Significance of Form in *Vanity Fair*." *PMLA* 82, no. 7 (1967): 530–41.

———. *Thackeray the Writer: From Journalism to "Vanity Fair."* New York: Macmillan, 1998.

Hassan, Ihab. "Quest for the Subject: The Self in Literature." *Contemporary Literature* 29, no. 3 (1988): 420–37.

Helm, Paul. "Pretending and Intending." *Analysis* 31, no. 4 (1971): 127–32.

Hergenhan, L. T. "Meredith Achieves Recognition: The Reception of *Beauchamp's Career* and *The Egoist*." *Texas Studies in Literature and Language* 11 (1969): 1247–68.

———. "Meredith's Attempts to Win Popularity: Contemporary Reactions." *Studies in English Literature* 4, no. 4 (1964): 637–51.

Hume, David. *A Treatise of Human Nature.* Edited by David Fate Norton and Mary J. Norton. New York: Oxford University Press, 2000.

Jain, Krishna. *Description in Philosophy.* Bali Nagar: D. K. Printworld, 1994.

Keefe, Rosanna, and Peter Smith. Introduction to *Vagueness: A Reader.* Edited by Rosanna Keefe and Peter Smith, 1–57. Cambridge, MA: MIT Press, 1999.

Kellman, Steven G. "Raising the Net: Iris Murdoch and the Tradition of the Self-Begetting Novel." *English Studies* 57, no. 1 (1976): 43–50.

Kelly, Sean Dorrance. "Merleau-Ponty on the Body." *Ratio* 15, no. 4 (2002): 377–91.

———. *The Relevance of Phenomenology to the Philosophy of Language and Mind.* New York: Garland, 2001.

———. "Seeing Things in Merleau-Ponty." In *The Cambridge Companion to Merleau-Ponty*, edited by Taylor Carman and Mark B. N. Hansen, 74–110. New York: Cambridge University Press, 2005.

Kermode, Frank. "The House of Fiction." *Partisan Review* 30, no. 1 (1963): 61–82 .

Kim, Jaegwon. "Perception and Reference without Causality." *Journal of Philosophy* 74, no. 10 (1977): 606–620.

———. *Supervenience and Mind.* New York: Cambridge University Press, 1993.

Knapp, Steven, and Walter Benn Michaels. "Against Theory." *Critical Inquiry* 8, no. 4 (1982): 723–42.

Knights, L. C. "The Grounds of Literary Criticism." *Neophilologus* 40, no. 1 (1956): 207–15.

Kripke, Saul. *Naming and Necessity.* Cambridge, MA: Harvard University Press, 1980.

Kroon, Frederick. "Millian Descriptivism." *Australasian Journal of Philosophy* 82, no. 4 (2004): 553–76.

Kurnick, David. "Empty Houses: Thackeray's Theater of Interiority." *Victorian Studies* 48, no. 2 (2006): 257–67.

Lamarque, Peter. "Bits and Pieces of Fiction." *British Journal of Aesthetics* 24, no. 1 (1984): 53–58.

———. "Truth and Art in Iris Murdoch's *The Black Prince.*" *Philosophy and Literature* 2, no. 2 (1978): 202–22.

———, and Stein Haugom Olsen, eds. *Aesthetics and the Philosophy of Art: The Analytic Tradition.* New York: Blackwell, 2004.

Leavis, L. R. "The Anti-Artist: The Case of Iris Murdoch." *Neophilologus* 72, no. 1 (1988): 139.

Levine, Caroline. *Forms: Whole, Rhythm, Hierarchy, Network.* Cambridge, MA: Harvard University Press, 2014.

Levine, George. *The Realistic Imagination: English Fiction from Frankenstein to Lady Chatterley.* Chicago: University of Chicago Press, 1981.

Levinson, Jerrold. "What a Musical Work Is." In Lamarque and Olsen, *Aesthetics and the Philosophy of Art*, 78–91.

Lewes, George Henry. Review of *Vanity Fair*, by William Makepeace Thackeray. *Athenaeum* 1085 (August 12, 1848): 794–97.

———. *Studies in Animal Life.* New York: Harper and Bros., 1860.

Lewis, David. "Humean Supervenience." In *Philosophical Papers II*, ix–x. New York: Oxford University Press, 1986.

———. "Humean Supervenience Debugged." *Mind* 103, no. 412 (October 1994): 473–90.

———. "Many, but Almost One." In *Ontology, Causality and Mind*, edited by David Malet Armstrong, John Bacon, Keith Campbell, and Lloyd Reinhardt, 283–38. Cambridge: Cambridge University Press, 1993.

———. "New Work for a Theory of Universals." *Australasian Journal of Philosophy* 62 (1984): 343–77.

———. *On the Plurality of Worlds.* Oxford: Blackwell, 1986.

———. "Reduction of Mind." In *A Companion to the Philosophy of Mind*, edited by S. Guttenplan, 419–20. London: Blackwell, 1994.

———. "Scorekeeping in a Language Game." *Journal of Philosophical Logic* 8 (1979): 339–59.

Litvak, Joseph. *Strange Gourmets.* Durham, NC: Duke University Press, 1997.

Locke, John. *An Essay Concerning Human Understanding.* Oxford: Clarendon Press, 1894.

Loeffler, Ronald. "Normative Phenomenalism: On Robert Brandom's Practice-Based Explanation of Meaning." *European Journal of Philosophy* 13, no. 1 (2005): 32–69.

Lynch, Deidre. *The Economy of Character.* Chicago: University of Chicago Press, 1998.

Lupton, Christina. "Theorizing Surfaces and Depths: Gaskell's *Cranford*." *Criticism* 50, no. 2 (2008): 235–54.

Marin, Louis. *The Semiotics of the Passion Narrative.* Translated by Alfred M. Johnson. Thomastown, Australia: Pickwick Press, 2004.

McCuskey, Brian. "Fetishizing the Flunkey: Thackeray and the Uses of Deviance." *Novel* 32, no. 3 (1999): 384–400.

Meiland, Jack W. "Originals, Copies, and Aesthetic Value." In Lamarque and Olsen, *Aesthetics and the Philosophy of Art*, 375–83.

Meredith, George. *The Amazing Marriage.* New York: Scribner's, 1895.

———. *The Egoist.* Edited by Robert M. Adams. New York: W. W. Norton, 1979.

Merleau-Ponty, Maurice. *Husserl at the Limits of Phenomenology.* Edited and translated by Leonard Lawlor and Bettina Bergo. Evanston, IL: Northwestern University Press, 2002.

———. *The Phenomenology of Perception.* Translated by Colin Smith. New York: Routledge, 2003.

Metzinger, Thomas. *Being No One: The Self-Model Theory of Subjectivity.* Cambridge, MA: MIT Press, 2001.

Michta, Natalie Cole. "The Legitimate Self in George Meredith's *Evan Harrington*." *Studies in the Novel* 21, no. 1 (1989): 41–60.

Mill, John Stuart. *A System of Logic.* Honolulu, University Press of the Pacific, 2002.

Miller, Andrew H. "The Fragments and Small Opportunities of *Cranford*." *Genre* 25, no. 1 (1992): 91–111.

————. *Novels Behind Glass.* New York: Cambridge University Press, 1995.

Miller, J. Hillis. *The Form of Victorian Fiction.* Notre Dame, IN: University of Notre Dame Press, 1968.

————. "'Herself Against Herself': The Clarification of Clara Middleton." In *The Representation of Women in Fiction*, edited by Carolyn G. Heilbrun and Margaret R. Higonnet, 98–123. Baltimore, MD: Johns Hopkins University Press, 1983.

————. *Reading Narrative.* Norman: University of Oklahoma Press, 1998.

————. "Trollope's Thackeray." *Nineteenth-Century Fiction* 37, no. 3 (1982): 350–57.

Millgram, Elijah, ed. *Varieties of Practical Reasoning.* Cambridge, MA: MIT Press, 2001.

Mitchell, W. J. T. "Wittgenstein's Imagery and What It Tells Us." *New Literary History* 19, no. 2 (1988): 361–70.

Moran, Richard. "The Expression of Feeling in Imagination." *Philosophical Review* 103, no. 1 (1994): 75–106.

Morris, Christopher. "Hands Around: Image and Theme in *The Egoist.*" *ELH* 34, no. 3 (1967): 367–79.

————. "Richard Feveral and the Fictional Lineage of Desire." *ELH* 42, no. 2 (1975): 242–57.

Murdoch, Iris. "Against Dryness." *Encounter* 16, no. 1 (1961): 16–20.

————. "The Idea of Perfection." In *The Sovereignty of Good.* New York: Routledge, 1970.

————. Interview by Michael O. Bellamy. *Contemporary Literature* 18, no. 2 (1977): 129–40.

————. Interview by S. B. Sagare. *Modern Fiction Studies* 47, no. 3 (2001): 696–714.

————. "Literature and Philosophy: A Conversation with Bryan Magee." In *Existentialists and Mystics: Writings on Philosophy and Literature*, edited by Peter Conradi. New York: Penguin, 1997.

————. *Metaphysics as a Guide to Morals.* New York: Penguin, 1992.

————. *Nuns and Soldiers.* New York: Penguin, 2002.

————. *The Red and the Green.* New York: Penguin, 1988.

————. "The Sublime and the Beautiful Revisited." *Yale Review* 49 (December 1959): 247–71.

———. "The Sublime and the Good." *Chicago Review* 13, no. 3 (1959): 42–55.

———. *Under the Net.* New York: Penguin, 1982.

———. "Vision and Choice in Morality." *Proceedings of the Aristotelian Society, Supplementary Volumes* 30 (1956): 32–58.

Myers, William. *The Presence of Persons.* London: Ashgate, 1998.

Ngai, Sianne. *Ugly Feelings.* Cambridge, MA: Harvard University Press, 2005.

Nussbaum, Martha. "Faint with Secret Knowledge: Love and Vision in Murdoch's *The Black Prince.*" *Poetics Today* 25, no. 4 (2004): 689–710.

———. *Upheavals of Thought.* New York: Cambridge University Press, 2001.

O'Grady, Paul. "Anscombe on the Tractatus." *Philosophy* 71, no. 276 (1996): 297–303.

Perkins, F. B. and Hippolyte Taine. *Charles Dickens: A Sketch of His Life and Works.* New York, G. P. Putnam and Sons, 1870.

Plotz, John. *Portable Property: Victorian Culture on the Move.* Princeton, NJ: Princeton University Press, 2008.

Pritchett, V. S. *George Meredith and English Comedy.* London: Chatto and Windus, 1970.

Putnam, Hilary. "Is There a Fact of the Matter about Fiction?" *Poetics Today* 4, no. 1 (1983): 77–81.

———. "Meaning and Reference." *Journal of Philosophy* 70, no. 19 (1973): 699–711.

Quine, W. V. O. *From a Logical Point of View.* Cambridge, MA: Harvard University Press, 1961.

———. *Ontological Relativity and Other Essays.* New York: Columbia University Press, 1969.

———. *Word and Object.* Cambridge, MA: MIT Press, 1960.

Reimer, Marga. "Demonstrating with Descriptions." *Philosophy and Phenomenological Research* 52, no. 4 (1992): 877–93.

———"Quotation Marks: Demonstratives or Demonstrations?" *Analysis* 56, no. 3 (1996): 131–41.

———. "Reference." In *The Stanford Encyclopedia of Philosophy*, edited by Edward N. Zalta. Stanford, CA: Stanford University Press 2003. Online at <http://plato.stanford.edu/entries/reference/>.

———, and Anne Bezuidenhout. *Descriptions and Beyond.* New York: Oxford, 2004.

Ricoeur, Paul. "Greimas's Narrative Grammar." Translated by Frank Collins and Paul Perron. *New Literary History* 20, no. 3 (1989): 581–608.

———. "The Metaphorical Process as Cognition, Imagination, and Feeling." *Critical Inquiry* 5, no. 1 (1978): 143–59.

Rigby, Elizabeth. Review of *Vanity Fair*, by William Makepeace Thackeray. *Quarterly Review* 84, no. 167 (1848).

Risjord, Mark. "Reasons, Causes, and Action Explanation." *Philosophy of the Social Sciences* 35, no. 3 (2005): 294–306.

Ritchie, Anne Thackeray. Introduction to *The Memoirs of Barry Lyndon, Esq*. In *The Biographical Edition of W. M. Thackeray's Complete Works*, edited by Anne Thackeray Ritchie, xxxiii–xxxiv. New York: Harper and Bros., 1898.

Romberg, Bertil. *Studies in the Narrative Technique of the First-Person Novel*. Stockholm: Almqvist and Wiksell, 1962.

Rumfitt, Ian. "Frege's Theory of Predication: An Elaboration and Defense, with Some New Applications." *Philosophical Review* 103, no. 4 (1994): 599–637.

Russell, Bertrand. *Introduction to Mathematical Philosophy*. London: George Allen and Unwin, 1919.

———. *Introduction to Mathematical Philosophy*. New York: Routledge, 1993.

———. Introduction to *Tractatus Logico-Philosophicus*, ix–xxv. Translated by D. F. Pears and B. F. McGuinness. New York: Routledge, 2001.

———. *The Philosophy of Logical Atomism*. New York: Open Court, 1985.

Sainsbury, R. M. Review of *The Varieties of Reference*, by Gareth Evans. *Mind* 94 (1985): 120–42.

———, and David Wiggins. "Names, Fictional Names, and 'Really.'" *Proceedings of the Aristotelian Society Supplement* 73, no. 1 (1999): 271–86.

Sassoon, Siegfried. *Meredith*. London: Constable, 1948.

Scarry, Elaine. *Dreaming by the Book*. Princeton, NJ: Princeton University Press, 1999.

———. *Resisting Representation*. New York: Oxford University Press, 1994.

Schiffer, Stephen. "The Basis of Reference." *Erkenntnis* 13 (1978): 171–206.

————. Review of *The Varieties of Reference*, by Gareth Evans. *Journal of Philosophy* 85, no. 1 (1988): 33–42.

Searle, John. *Intentionality*. New York: Cambridge, 1983.

————. "The Logical Status of Fictional Discourse." *New Literary History* 6, no. 2 (1975): 319–32.

Shier, David. "How Can Pictures Be Propositions?" *Ratio* 10, no. 1 (1997): 65–75.

Simpson, David. "Lying, Liars and Language." *Philosophy and Phenomenological Research* 52, no. 3 (1992): 623–39.

Smirlock, Daniel. "Rough Truth: Synecdoche and Interpretation in *The Egoist*." *Nineteenth-Century Fiction* 31, no. 3 (1976): 313–28.

Smith, Jonathan. "'The Cock of Lordly Plume': Sexual Selection and *The Egoist*." *Nineteenth-Century Literature* 50, no. 1 (1995): 51–77.

Sosa, David. "Checking Searle's Background." *Teorema* 18, no. 1 (1999): 109–10.

Stalnaker, Robert C. *Ways a World Might Be*. New York: Cambridge University Press, 2003.

Stanley, Jason. "Context and Logical Form." *Linguistics and Philosophy* 23 (2000): 391–434.

————, and Timothy Williamson. "Quantifiers and Context-Dependence." *Analysis* 55, no. 4 (1995): 291–95.

Stanzel, Franz K. "Second Thoughts on Narrative Situations in the Novel: Towards a 'Grammar of Fiction.'" *Novel* 11, no. 3 (1978): 247–64.

Stephen, James Fitzjames. Review of *Barry Lyndon*, by William Makepeace Thackeray. In *Thackeray: The Critical Heritage*, ed. Geoffrey Tillotson and Donald Hawes. New York: Barnes and Noble, 1968. Orig. pub. in the *Saturday Review*, December 1856.

Stewart, Maaja A. "The Country House Ideals in Meredith's *The Egoist*." *Nineteenth-Century Fiction* 32, no. 4 (1978): 420–41.

Strawson, P. F. "Identifying Reference" In *Logico-Linguistic Papers*, 75–95. London: Ashgate, 2004.

————. "On Referring." *Mind* 59, no. 235 (1950): 135–60.

Sudrann, Jean. "'The Linked Eye and Mind': A Concept of Action in the Novels of George Meredith." *Studies in English Literature* 4, no. 4 (1964): 617–35.

Taube, Myron. "Thackeray and the Reminiscential Vision." *Nineteenth-Century Fiction* 18, no. 3 (1963): 247–59.

Taylor, Charles. "Merleau-Ponty and the Epistemological Picture." In *The Cambridge Companion to Merleau-Ponty*, edited by Taylor Carman and Mark B. N. Hansen, 26–57. New York: Cambridge University Press, 2005.

Thackeray, William Makepeace. "Autour de mon chapeau." In *The Roundabout Papers*. New York: Houghton, Mifflin, 1889.

———. *The Book of Snobs*. Köln: Könemann, 1999.

———. *Catherine*. Ann Arbor: University of Michigan Press, 1999.

———. *The Irish Sketch Book*. London: Smith Elder, 1887.

———. *The Letters and Private Papers of William Makepeace Thackeray*. Edited by Gordon N. Ray. 4 vols. Cambridge, MA: Harvard University Press, 1946.

———. *The Luck of Barry Lyndon*. Edited by Edgar F. Harden. Ann Arbor: University of Michigan Press, 1999.

———. *The Memoirs of Barry Lyndon, Esq.* Edited by Andrew Sanders. Oxford: Oxford University Press, 1999.

———. *Pendennis*. London: J. M. Dent, 1910.

———. *Vanity Fair*. Edited by John Sutherland. Oxford: Oxford University Press, 1983.

———. *Vanity Fair*. Edited by J. I. M. Stewart. New York: Penguin, 1985.

———. *Vanity Fair*. Edited by Peter L. Shillingsburg. New York: W. W. Norton, 1994.

Thalberg, Irving. "Singling Out Actions: Their Properties and Components." *Journal of Philosophy* 68, no. 20 (1971): 781–87.

Theobald, D. W. "Philosophy and Fiction." *British Journal of Aesthetics* 14, no. 1 (1974): 17–25.

Thompson, Judith Jarvis. "Individuating Actions." *Journal of Philosophy* 68, no. 20 (1971): 774–81.

Tillotson, Geoffrey, and Donald Hawes, eds. *Thackeray: The Critical Heritage*. New York: Barnes and Noble, 1968.

Todorov, Tzvetan. "Reading as Construction." In *Essentials of the Theory of Fiction*, edited by Michael J. Hoffman and Patrick D. Murphy, 157–58. Durham, NC: Duke University Press, 2005.

Travis, Charles. "Classical Theories of Reference." In "Supplementary Volume 6: New Essays in Philosophy of Language." Special issue, *Canadian Journal of Philosophy* 10, supp. 1 (1980): 139–59.

Trollope, Anthony. *Thackeray*. London: Macmillan, 1879.

Van Ghent, Dorothy. *The English Novel: Form and Function*. New York: Harper, 1953.

Vogler, Candace. "Anscombe on Practical Inference." In *Varieties of Practical Reasoning*, edited by Elijah Millgram, 438–64. Cambridge, MA: MIT Press, 2001.

———. *Reasonably Vicious*. Cambridge, MA: Harvard University Press, 2002.

Wagner, Valeria. *Bound to Act*. Stanford, CA: Stanford University Press, 1999.

Walton, Kendall. *Mimesis as Make-Believe*. Cambridge, MA: Harvard University Press, 1990.

Watson, George. "Iris Murdoch and the Net of Theory." *Hudson Review* 51, no. 3 (1998): 490–500.

Watson, John. "Thackeray's Composite Characters in *Barry Lyndon*." *Journal of the Australasian Universities Language and Literature Association* 87, no. 1 (1997): 25–42.

Weil, Simone. *Gravity and Grace*. New York: Routledge, 2002.

Wheatley, James H. *Patterns in Thackeray's Fiction*. Cambridge, MA: MIT Press, 1969.

White, Allon. *The Uses of Obscurity*. Boston: Routledge and Kegan Paul, 1981.

Widmann, R. L. "Murdoch's *Under the Net*: Theory and Practice of Fiction." *Critique* 10, no. 1 (1967): 5–16.

Wilde, Oscar. "The Decay of Lying." In *The Complete Works of Oscar Wilde*. Edited by Vyvyan Holland. New York: Harper and Row, 1989, 970–992.

Williams, Carolyn. "Unbroken Patternes: Gender, Culture, and Voice in *The Egoist*." *Browning Institute Studies* 13 (1985): 45–70.

Williams, Ioan M. *Meredith: The Critical Heritage*. New York: Barnes and Noble, 1971.

Williamson, Timothy. *Knowledge and Its Limits*. Oxford: Clarendon, 2000.

———. "Wright on the Epistemic Conception of Vagueness." *Analysis* 56, no. 1 (1996): 39–45.

Wimsatt W. K., and Monroe C. Beardsley, "The Intentional Fallacy." In *Critical Theory Since Plato*, edited by Hazard Adams, 1014–31. New York: Harcourt Brace Jovanovich, 1971.

Wittgenstein, Ludwig. *Culture and Value*. Translated by Peter Winch.

Edited by G. H. Von Wright. Chicago: University of Chicago Press, 1984.

———. *Philosophical Investigations.* Translated and edited by G. E. M. Anscombe. Oxford: Blackwell, 2001.

———. *Tractatus Logico-Philosophicus.* Translated by D. F. Pears and B. F. McGuinness. New York: Routledge 2001.

Wollheim, Richard. "On Pictorial Representation." In Lamarque and Olsen, *Aesthetics and the Philosophy of Art*, 396–406.

Woloch, Alex. *The One vs. the Many.* Princeton, NJ: Princeton University Press, 2003.

Wong, Kai-Yee. "*A Priority* and Ways of Grasping a Proposition." *Philosophical Studies* 62, no. 2 (1991): 151–64.

Woolf, Virginia. *The Essays of Virginia Woolf.* Vol. 3. Edited by Andrew McNellie. New York: Harcourt Brace Jovanovich, 1988.

———. *The Common Reader.* New York: Harcourt Brace, 1925.

———. "The Patron and the Crocus," in Woolf, *Common Reader*, 206–211.

Wrathall, Mark, and Jeff Malpas, eds. *Heidegger, Coping, and Cognitive Science.* Cambridge, MA: MIT Press, 2000.

Zalta, Edward N. "Referring to Fictional Characters." *Dialectica* 57, no. 2 (2003): 243–54.

Žižek, Slavoj. *The Parallax View.* Cambridge, MA: MIT Press, 2006.

Index